AF324847

Examinations in Singapore
Change and Continuity
(1891–2007)

Examinations in Singapore
Change and Continuity
(1891–2007)

Tan Yap Kwang
Chow Hong Kheng
Christine Goh

Singapore Examinations and Assessment Board

NEW JERSEY · LONDON · SINGAPORE · BEIJING · SHANGHAI · HONG KONG · TAIPEI · CHENNAI

Published by

World Scientific Publishing Co. Pte. Ltd.

5 Toh Tuck Link, Singapore 596224

USA office: 27 Warren Street, Suite 401-402, Hackensack, NJ 07601

UK office: 57 Shelton Street, Covent Garden, London WC2H 9HE

British Library Cataloguing-in-Publication Data
A catalogue record for this book is available from the British Library.

EXAMINATIONS IN SINGAPORE
Change and Continuity (1891–2007)

ISBN-13 978-981-279-413-0
ISBN-10 981-279-413-1

Typeset by Lab Creations

Printed by Fuisland offset Pte Ltd, Singapore.

The raison d'être for a historical account of examinations in Singapore is organisational and professional in origin and intent.

One, the Singapore Examinations and Assessment Board (SEAB), as a new statutory board, is established to take greater control of the national examination system and positioned as a centre for testing and assessment services in the region and beyond, capitalising on the strong international standing of Singapore's education system. As national examinations are our core business, a broad understanding of how the present state of examinations came to be is sine qua non.

Two, it is timely to take stock of examinations in Singapore in view of the recent 50th anniversary of the Ministry of Education (1957–2007) and the 150th anniversary of the University of Cambridge Local Examinations Syndicate (1858–2008).

Three, few studies focus on examinations per se. The reason is perhaps obvious, as examinations are outcomes of the political, economic and social agendas of the respective governing authority (British colonial government, Japanese military administration and independent Singapore government) and the consequent policies for education. Yet, it is interesting to study the historical momentum of examinations, with changes and

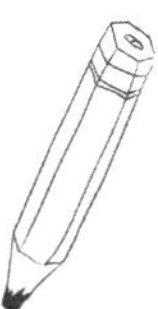

continuities in examinations in the foreground and broader history of Singapore and of education in Singapore in the background.

This historical survey of examinations is indebted to earlier studies on education from the founding of Singapore up to recent times. David D. Chelliah, Theodore R. Doraisamy, Francis Wong Hoy Kee and Gwee Yee Hean, H. A. Wyndham and Harold E. Wilson presented invaluable insights into vernacular and English education; and Theodore R. Doraisamy and John Yip Soon Kwong and Sim Wong Kooi provided a broad survey of educational developments and policies up to recent times.

In addition, this historical account hopes to contribute perspectives arising from primary documents from the National Archives of Singapore, the Lee Kong Chian Reference Library and the Cambridge Assessment Archives. Local sources include Straits Settlements Legislative Council Papers and the Annual Reports of the Department of Education/Ministry of Education, oral history interviews, amongst others. Cambridge sources include: the letter from the Reverend G. F. Browne on the setting up of an examination centre in Singapore, documents related to the Sime Road Camp School Certificate examination, Annual Reports of the University of Cambridge Local Examinations Syndicate, past question papers, colonial class lists, amongst others.

This book adopts the approach of an examination question paper in constructing a chronological account of examinations. It poses questions on the key milestones of examinations and suggests answers to help readers unravel the changes and continuities of examinations in Singapore. The historical study of examinations is juxtaposed against its immediate context of education and wider context of politics, economy and society. This study covers three broad historical periods: Examinations in Singapore (1891–1945), The Post War Years (1946–1970s) and Charting Our Destiny (1980s –2007). In the British period up to 1941, local examinations were conducted by the vernacular schools, and external examinations by the University of Cambridge Local Examinations Syndicate. There was a lack of systematic effort to establish a uniform system of education and examinations. During the Japanese Occupation, examinations were conducted by the Japanese authorities and, unexpectedly, the Cambridge examinations continued in the Sime Road Camp. In the post-war period, and particularly after Singapore was granted self-government, the establishment of a national education system was followed by the emergence of national examinations: the Primary School Leaving Examinations and the Singapore-Cambridge GCE N/O/A Levels for every school-going child in Singapore. Thereafter, the nature of national examinations evolved with the changing needs of education and the nation. At the turn of the century, with the Ministry of Education's decision to take greater control of examinations, SEAB was established to oversee new developments in examinations.

ACKNOWLEDGEMENTS

To the following, the authors would like to express their heartfelt gratitude:

Miss Seah Jiak Choo, Director-General of Education, for inspiring in us the idea of a historical account of examinations within the larger context of the history of education, and in doing so, motivate us to contemplate on the changes and continuities in examinations.

Cambridge Assessment, for contributing pivotal primary documents that became historical anchors from the onset of conceptualisation of this project. one, the Reverend G. F. Browne's letter on the setting up of an examination centre in the Straits Settlements; and two, documents related to the Sime Road Camp School Certificate examination. Special thanks to Cambridge Assessment Group Archivist Ms Gillian Cooke for facilitating our research at the Cambridge Assessment Archives and sharing numerous primary documents relating to Cambridge examinations in Singapore.

National Archives of Singapore, for primary documents dating from the Straits Settlements days and oral history sources. Special thanks to Ms Yvonne Chan and Mrs Wong-Yap Hwai Fey for advising on the use of archival sources and facilitating our research.

Lee Kong Chian Reference Library, for the good collection of books on Singapore's history that has enabled us to bridge gaps of time and place. Special thanks to Ms Azizah Sidek whose expertise on sources relating to the history of Singapore has given us access to significant primary and secondary sources.

Our SEAB colleagues who have contributed to this project, particularly Mr Raymond Lim, Mr Rick Lim and Ms Connie Ang. Special thanks to Mr Koh Hoe Kuan, truly an 'insider' to the developments in examinations, for sharing his personal experience and collection of old documents for this project.

World Scientific, our publisher who has generously supported our project to share the history of examinations with the education fraternity and the public at large. Special thanks to Ms Teng Poh Hoon for her editorial work in support of the publication of this book.

Last but not least, this book is dedicated to all in the education fraternity who are truly participants and witnesses to the changes and continuities in the history of education and examinations and to all interested readers.

B The Post-War Years (1946–1970s)   53

C Charting Our Destiny (1980s–2007)   107

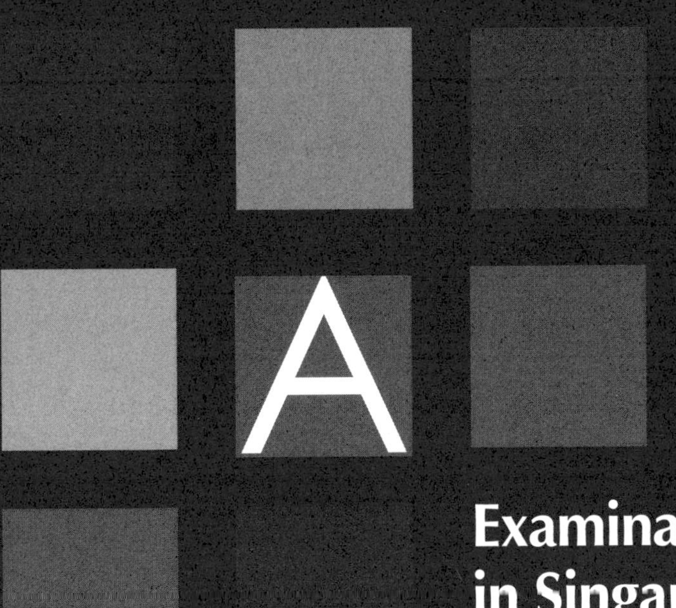

Examinations in Singapore

(1891 – 1945)

CHAPTER

Trace the development of examinations in Singapore during the British colonial period up to 1941.

We [the University of Cambridge Local Examinations Syndicate] shall be glad to form a centre at Singapore. It will be quite satisfactory to us that the management of the examination should be in the hands of the officers of the Education Department of the Colony.[1]

Reverend G. F. Browne (1891)

And thus began a relationship between the University of Cambridge Local Examinations Syndicate (UCLES) and Singapore that continues to this day. This relationship laid the foundation for the national system of education and examinations as we know it today.

BEGINNINGS OF EDUCATION IN A PLURAL SOCIETY

In 1819, the British East India Company (EIC) established a trading post in Singapore. As the EIC's interest in Singapore was primarily commercial, scant attention was paid to education. This was despite Raffles' humanitarian and liberal view that education 'must keep pace with commerce in order that its benefits may be assured and its evil avoided'.[2] Raffles had intended '...to afford the means of education in the Native languages to such of the Company's servants and others as they may desire it'.[3]

---

[1] Letter from the Reverend G. F. Browne, Secretary of the University of Cambridge Local Examinations Syndicate to Sir C. C. Smith, Governor of the Straits Settlements, 8 July 1891, *Cambridge Assessment Archives Service Examination Letter Books A/LB 1/2, Volume II, Dec 1890– Dec 1891*, UK: University of Cambridge Local Examinations Syndicate.

[2] H. A. Wyndham, *Problems of Imperial Trusteeship. Native Education. Ceylon, Java, Formosa, the Philippines, French Indo-China, and British Malaya*, London: Oxford University Press, 1933, p. 221.

[3] "Annual Report of 1856", in *Annual Reports of the Straits Settlements 1855–1941*, Singapore: National Archives of Singapore, p. 13.

As Singapore's geographic position and system of free trade predisposed it as a port of exchange,[4] it became an attractive migrant destination. In a relatively short period of time, Singapore became a plural society made up of diverse migrant populations — the Malays from different parts of the Malay Archipelago, the Chinese mainly from Southern China with various dialect groups, and the Indians hailing from various parts of India. This then resulted in the development of vernacular schools by the different local communities.

Up to 1867, the British government therefore did not control English or vernacular education and contented itself with subsidising a few schools.[5] The schools were left unchecked, without any form of government supervision.

From 1867, Singapore came under the direct rule of the Colonial Office in London as part of the Straits Settlements. In 1870, Sir Henry Ord, the first Governor of the Straits Settlements, appointed Colonel R. Woolley to enquire into the state of education. Woolley recommended two courses of action to improve the 'backward' state of education in the Straits Settlements: one, to begin de novo and thoroughly re-organise all existing educational establishments; and two, to take the schools as they were, and by a gradual process, endeavour to place them on a more satisfactory and improved basis.[6] Whilst the British preferred not to upset what was status quo, they saw the need to exert some form of control over education in the colony with the appointment of Mr A. M. Skinner as Inspector of Schools in the newly created Department of Education in 1872.[7]

[4] H. A. Wyndham, *Problems of Imperial Trusteeship. Native Education. Ceylon, Java, Formosa, the Philippines, French Indo-China, and British Malaya*, London: Oxford University Press, 1933, p. 197.

[5] Ibid., p. 199.

[6] "Report of the Select Committee of the Legislative Council to enquire into the state of education in the Colony (The Woolley Report), 1870" in Francis H. K. Wong & Y. H. Gwee, *Official Reports on Education: Straits Settlements and the Federated Malay States 1870–1939*, Singapore: Pan Pacific Book Distributors (S) Pte Ltd, 1980, p. 12.

[7] In 1901, the title of the Inspector of Schools was renamed Director of Public Instruction and in 1906, renamed Director of Education. The Director of Education was assisted by the Inspector of Schools for Singapore and Malacca and Inspector of Schools for Penang. In "Education of the Colony" *Straits Settlements Paper laid before the Legislative Council, 31 January 1913*, Singapore: National Archives of Singapore, p. 4.

EXAMINATIONS IN ENGLISH STREAM SCHOOLS

The English stream schools were attended by all races, with English language as the medium of instruction. There were two categories of English stream schools: one, the 'free' schools which later became government schools, such as Singapore Free School (1834) that later became Raffles Institution (1868), Raffles Girls' School (1844), Victoria Bridge School (1906); and two, grant-in-aid private boys' schools founded by Christian missionary organisations such as St. Joseph Institution (1852), Anglo-Chinese School (1886), Anglo-Chinese Free School (1893), St. Anthony's School (1879), St. Andrew's Mission School (1890), Anglo-Tamil School, and grant-in-aid private girls' schools such as Convent School (1851), St. Anthony Girls' School (1879), American Mission Girls' School, American Mission Chinese Girls School and Singapore Chinese Girls' School (1899).[8] Most of these schools received grants-in-aid from the British government. In the period from 1819 to 1867, however, there were no government English schools.[9]

The British government took deliberate steps to promote English as the medium of instruction as it was the language of the colonial government and administration. Government grants favoured schools that imparted English to pupils whose home language was not English. These grants were based on pupils' achievement in English. Moreover, pupils must obtain a full pass in English before they could be presented for examination in an extra subject outside the curriculum.[10] The great demand for English stream qualifications was also due to the marked wage difference between English versus vernacular-educated boys.[11]

English stream schools, supported by a systematic organisation of English stream examinations, emerged as having the most structured system of education vis-à-vis the vernacular schools. They were organised according to six standards and requirements laid down for each standard. These schools provided 11 years of education — primary school (Primary I, II & Standard I), elementary school (Standard II–V)

---

[8] Ibid, pp.1–4.

[9] Theodore R. Doraisamy (ed.), *150 Years of Education in Singapore*, Singapore: Stamford College Press Ltd, 1969, p. 36.

[10] H. A. Wyndham, *Problems of Imperial Trusteeship. Native Education. Ceylon, Java, Formosa, the Philippines, French Indo-China, and British Malaya*, London: Oxford University Press, 1933, p. 203.

[11] Ibid.

and secondary school (Standard VI to IX), with the Cambridge School Certificate Examination taken at the end of Standard IX — the 九号 — 'jiuhao' in Mandarin, or the much-sought-after 'kow hor' in the Fujian (Hokkien) dialect.

Scholarship Examinations

The first external examinations emerged in 1863, with the first Competitive State Scholarship Examinations conducted by an 'Examination Board' that comprised the Resident Councillor and the 'Residency' Chaplain. The government had hoped that the scholarships would create a healthy spirit of rivalry among the schools and promote higher standards of education.[12]

In 1885, the Queen's scholarships were initiated by Sir Cecil Clementi Smith, Governor of the Straits Settlements.[13] It was first awarded in 1886, 'in order to allow promising boys an opportunity of completing their studies in England and to encourage a number of boys to remain in school and acquire a really useful education'.[14] Recipients of the scholarships would proceed to study at either Cambridge or Oxford Universities in the United Kingdom (UK).[15] Before the introduction of the Cambridge Local Examinations, preparation for these scholarship examinations was the only serious work undertaken for secondary education.[16] From 1897 to 1902, after the introduction of the Cambridge Local Examinations, the scholarships were awarded based on the results of the Senior Cambridge Examination. From 1903, the University of Cambridge conducted a special examination for candidates who had previously passed the Senior Cambridge Examination. In 1910, the scholarships were discontinued due to the following: one, the subjects of Latin, French and Mathematics were deemed to be not suited to local needs; two, scholarships led to unwholesome competition; and three, a few brilliant pupils benefited at the expense of the majority of the

[12] Theodore R. Doraisamy (ed.), *150 Years of Education in Singapore*, Singapore: Stamford College Press Ltd, 1969, p. 14.
[13] http://www.pscscholarships.gov.sg/SCHOLARSHIPS/Presidents_Scholarship.htm
[14] "Report of the Commission of Enquiry into the system of English education in the colony (the Kynnerseley Report), 1902" in Francis H. K. Wong & Y. H. Gwee, *Official Reports on Education: Straits Settlements and the Federated Malay States 1870–1939*, Singapore: Pan Pacific Book Distributors (s) Pte Ltd, 1980, p. 45.
[15] http://www.pscscholarships.gov.sg/SCHOLARSHIPS/Presidents_Scholarship.htm
[16] J. B. Neilson, *Annual Report of the Department of Education 1947*, Singapore: Government Printing Office, 1948, p. 7.

pupils.[17] However, in 1923, the scholarships were restored. In 1939, new regulations were introduced to limit scholarships to graduates from Raffles College and College of Medicine.[18]

The Queen's scholarships benefited a small minority of the English-educated population who were almost guaranteed of professional careers. From the period of 1886 to 1900, 29 men were awarded the scholarship — 5 became civil engineers, 5 were lawyers, 15 took up medicine, 2 meant to adopt education as a career, 1 had died and the occupation of 1 was unknown.[19] In more recent times, prominent recipients of the Queen's Scholarships in Singapore include the former Minister of Law, the late E. W. Barker, Professor Lim Pin, and Kwa Geok Choo (Mrs Lee Kuan Yew).[20]

The Queen's Scholarship was replaced by the Singapore State Scholarship in 1959, the Yang di-Pertuan Scholarship in 1964 and the present-day President's scholarship in 1966.[21]

Elementary School Examinations

From 1872, the Department of Education conducted annual examinations in government and grant-in-aid schools in line with the recommendations of the *Woolley Report* for regular examinations to be held 'of a most searching character' and progress reports to be submitted to the government.[22] Consequently, schools were obliged to present its pupils for annual examinations. The amount of government grants to schools was dependent on good results. In 1899, this system of 'payment by results' was replaced by 'payment by classification'. Four types of grants were available: special grants, salary grants, maintenance grants and grants on results of examinations.[23] In 1919, payment by classification was replaced by 'payment by estimates' which made up the difference between revenue from school fees and other sources and the approved expenditure of

[17] Ibid.
[18] Ibid.
[19] H. A. Wyndham, *Problems of Imperial Trusteeship. Native Education. Ceylon, Java, Formosa, the Philippines, French Indo-China, and British Malaya*, London: Oxford University Press, 1933, p. 203.
[20] http://www.pscscholarships.gov.sg/SCHOLARSHIPS/Presidents_Scholarship.htm
[21] Ibid.
[22] "Report of the Select Committee of the Legislative Council to enquire into the state of education in the Colony (The Woolley Report), 1870" in Francis H. K. Wong & Y. H. Gwee, *Official Reports on Education: Straits Settlements and the Federated Malay States 1870–1939*, Singapore: Pan Pacific Book Distributors (S) Pte Ltd, 1980, p. 13.
[23] Theodore R. Doraisamy (ed.), *150 Years of Education in Singapore*, Singapore: Stamford College Press Ltd, 1969, p. 27.

the school.[24] In 1908, the regular formal annual inspections to schools were replaced by frequent surprise visits in order to determine the proper grade.[25]

In Singapore, the grant-in-aid schools had performed very well during inspections, as indicated in the *Report on the Examinations of Grant-in-Aid Schools* in 1880[26] below.

Schools	Percentage of passes obtained at Inspection 1879, including those obtained by pupils who failed in a majority of subjects
Raffles Institution	84
Singapore Brothers	74
Chinese Mission	66
Penang Free School	63
Penang Brothers	67
Pulo Tikus	53
Tamil Mission	53
Malacca French Mission	51
Portuguese Mission – Bandar Ilir	58
Portuguese Mission – Trangkerah	69

Secondary School Examinations

Secondary education, provided only in certain elementary schools, consisted of classes preparing for the commerce examinations or Cambridge Local Examinations.[27]

Students in the commerce classes pursued the 'Commercial and Civil Service Course', comprising subjects such as English, General Knowledge, Arithmetic, Business Training, Book-Keeping, Shorthand and Geography in the first year, and the same subjects plus Typewriting in the second

---

[24] Ibid., p. 28.
[25] Ibid., p. 27.
[26] "Report on the examinations of the grant-in-aid schools" in *Straits Settlements Paper laid before the Legislative Council, 20 May 1880*, Singapore: National Archives of Singapore, p. 57.
[27] "Education of the Colony" *Straits Settlements Paper laid before the Legislative Council, 31 January 1913*, Singapore: National Archives of Singapore, p. 8.

year.[28] By 1916, arrangements were made for the commercial classes candidates to be examined locally for the London Chamber of Commerce examinations.[29]

Cambridge Examinations Comes to Singapore

Students interested in sitting the Cambridge Local Examinations studied the 'Scholarship (Preparatory) Course' for subjects examined. The Cambridge Local Examinations comprised the Cambridge Local Junior Examination (first year) and Cambridge Local Senior Examination (second year).

The first Cambridge Local Examinations were offered in Singapore by UCLES[30] in 1892.[31] Presently, a number of books on education had suggested 1891 as the first year of Cambridge examinations. Some primary documents from the Cambridge Assessment Archives have suggested 1892 as the first year of examinations. Firstly, in a letter dated July 1891, the Reverend G. F. Browne, Secretary of UCLES agreed to a request from Sir C. C. Smith, Governor of the Straits Settlements, to set up an examination centre in Singapore. 1891 would have been too late for registration of examinations in the same year. The same letter also mentioned that 'forms of entry will be sent out in the early part of 1892'.[32] Secondly, the *Thirty-Fifth Annual Report of the Syndicate* stated that the Straits Settlements was a new centre in the December 1892 examinations.[33] Thirdly, the first time a Straits Settlements candidate (from Penang) was listed in the *Colonial Class List*, was in the December 1892 List.[34]

---

[28] Ibid.

[29] "Governor's address before Annual Report of 1916" in *Annual Reports of the Straits Settlements 1855–1941*, Singapore: National Archives of Singapore, p. 109.

[30] UCLES was re-branded as Cambridge Assessment in 2005.

[31] The first year of examinations conducted by the UCLES in the UK was in 1858.

[32] Letter from the Reverend G. F. Browne, Secretary of the University of Cambridge Local Examinations Syndicate to Sir C. C. Smith, Governor of the Straits Settlements, 8 July 1891, in *Cambridge Assessment Archives Service Examination Letter Books A/LB 1/2, Volume II, Dec 1890–Dec 1891*, UK: University of Cambridge Local Examinations Syndicate.

[33] *The Thirty-Fifth Annual Report of the Syndicate, 11 Mar 1893*, UK: University of Cambridge Local Examinations Syndicate, 1893, p. V.

[34] *Colonial Class Lists of 1891 and 1892*, UK: University of Cambridge Local Examinations Syndicate.

Letter from the Reverend G. F. Browne, Secretary of UCLES (1870–1892), to Sir C. C. Smith, Governor of the Straits Settlements (1887–1893) on the setting up of an examination centre in Singapore. © **UCLES** [35]

8 July 1891

Sir

Lord Knutsford [36] *has sent to us a copy of your letter of 30 May 1891, number 239, respecting the establishment of Cambridge Local Examinations in the Straits Settlements Colony.*

We shall be glad to form a centre at Singapore. It will be quite satisfactory to us that the management of the examination should be in the hands of the officers of the Education Department of the Colony.

The papers of questions would be sent through the Colonial Office to any address of which you may inform us.

I am sending by this mail six copies of our regulations for 1891 in order that the Masters of the several schools may see the general line of the examination. The titles of the variable books and periods or portions of subjects are printed in italics. We send to the colonies in which there are examination centres a list of the books selected for the next year's examination by such a mail as to reach them early in December; by this means they are enabled to give an early order for books.

The suggestions made in paragraphs 3, 4, 5 and 6 of your memorandum appear to us quite suitable.

Forms of entry will be sent out in the early part of 1892.

I am, Sir, your very faithful servant.

G F Browne

His Excellency
Sir C. C. Smith

---

[35] Letter from the Reverend G. F. Browne, Secretary of the University of Cambridge Local Examinations Syndicate to Sir C. C. Smith, Governor of the Straits Settlements, 8 July 1891, in *Cambridge Assessment Archives Service Examination Letter Books A/LB 1/2, Volume II, Dec 1890–Dec 1891*, UK: University of Cambridge Local Examinations Syndicate.

[36] Henry Thurstan Holland, 1st Viscount Knutsford was the then Secretary of State for the Colonies.

© UCLES

The Reverend G. F. Browne's Chair

The Reverend G. F. Browne's Chair has belonged to the UCLES since 1880s. Cambridge Assessment presented the chair to the Singapore Examinations and Assessment Board (SEAB) on 15 Aug 2006, 'to celebrate an enduring and fruitful partnership, developing successful students in the past, present and future'.

The Cambridge Local Examinations in the Straits Settlements had started with the Junior and Senior Cambridge Examinations. The Junior Cambridge Examinations had ceased for Malayan candidates in 1939.[37] The old Junior Cambridge class was then renamed Standard VIII, with a special syllabus preparing for entry to the School Certificate (old Senior Cambridge class).[38]

The Cambridge examinations were not without criticisms. As early as 1902, the *Report of the Commission of Enquiry into the System of*

[37] *The Eighty-Second Annual Report of the Syndicate, 2 May 1940*, UK: University of Cambridge Local Examinations Syndicate, 1940, p. 3.
[38] J. B. Neilson, *Annual Report of the Department of Education 1947*, Singapore: Government Printing Office, 1948, p. 7.

Reverend G. F. Browne M.A. D.D. Fellow of St. Catharine's College, Disney Professor of Archaeology, 1887–1892, Bishop of Bristol, 1897–1914, UCLES General Secretary, 1870–1892 © UCLES

English Education in the Colony (the Kynnerseley Report) had reported on public opinions that the Cambridge Local Examinations should be discontinued:

> It is argued that boys who should be studying English and subjects which are likely to fit them for their future career here, are crammed in a number of subjects so that they may pass or get honours at the Cambridge examinations. The boys are encouraged, instead of learning a few things well, to take up a great number of subjects in which they are crammed. Many of

the subjects will be of no use to them afterwards and owing to the
way they are learnt they cannot be of any practical value.[39]

Nonetheless, the report acknowledged the distinct improvement in
the standard of English education as a direct result of the Cambridge
examinations and was of the opinion that a local certificate would not
have the same value as the Cambridge certificate.[40]

The Cambridge Local Examinations also catered to the particular needs
of Malaya, by introduction of Special English and other papers, and
inclusion of local oriental languages as accepted second languages.[41]
In 1920, Malay was included in the syllabuses for the Junior and Senior
Examinations at Malayan centres.[42] By 1927, there were no fewer than
12 Asiatic languages amongst the subjects of the examination.[43]

**Excerpts from the 1892 Junior and Senior Cambridge Examination
Papers**

1892 Junior Cambridge Examination[44]

English Grammar (Tuesday, 13 December, 1892) © UCLES

A1. Define Abstract Noun; and give the derivation of the term abstract.
Form an Abstract Noun from (1) an Adjective, (2) a Verb, (3) a Common
Noun.

B1. Give a definition of the Subjunctive Mood, distinguishing it from the
Indicative. Illustrate this difference by sentences beginning with the
word "whether."
In what Mood is the word *may* in
(a)   You *may* go.
(b)   I give that you *may* give.
(c)   *May* good digestion wait on appetite.
Give reasons for your answer in each case.

[39] "Report of the Commission of Enquiry into the system of English education in the Colony (the
Kynnerseley Report), 1902" in Francis H. K. Wong & Y. H. Gwee, *Official Reports on Education:
Straits Settlements and the Federated Malay States 1870–1939*, Singapore: Pan Pacific Book
Distributors (S) Pte Ltd, 1980, p. 45.
[40] Ibid.
[41] J. B. Neilson, *Annual Report of the Department of Education 1947*, Singapore: Government Printing
Office, 1948, p. 7.
[42] *Syndicate Minutes*, 28 April 1920, Para 17, UK: University of Cambridge Local Examinations
Syndicate, p. 143.
[43] *The Seventieth Annual Report of the Syndicate, 1928*, UK: University of Cambridge Local
Examinations Syndicate, 1928.
[44] *Examination Papers 1892*, Junior Students, UK: University of Cambridge Local Examinations
Syndicate, 1892. © UCLES

C1. Write a sentence containing two extensions of the Predicate, and let one of these contain an Object with two enlargements of different kinds.

Arithmetic (Wednesday, 14 December, 1892) © UCLES

A1. Divide 16316316 by 163, and find the sum of the quotient and the remainder.

A2. A sum of £10. 19s. 9¼d. has to be divided equally among 137 people; how much does each receive?

B1. Find by Practice the value of 48 miles 5 furlongs 29 poles 3 yards of telegraph cable at £198 a mile.

B6. The French Railway Companies have recently reduced their rates for passengers as follows: 10 per cent. reduction on the old first class fares, 20 per cent. on the second class, and 30 per cent. on the third class fares. In consequence of this reduction they anticipate an increase in the number of people travelling per mile as follows: an increase of 15 per cent. in the number of first class passengers, 25 per cent. in the second class, and 40 per cent. in the third class. How much will the Railway Companies gain or lose per cent. on each class?

1892 Senior Cambridge Examination[45]

English Grammar (Tuesday, 13 December, 1892) © UCLES

A1. ANALYSE (in tabular form): -
She ceased, and Paris held the costly fruit
Out at arm's-length, so much the thought of power
Flattered his spirit: but Pallas, where she stood
Somewhat apart, her clear and bare *limbs*
O'erthwarted with the brazen-headed spear
Upon her pearly shoulder *leaning cold*,
The *while*, above, her full and earnest eye
Over her snow-cold breast and angry cheek
Kept watch, *waiting* decision, made reply.

A2. Parse the words in italics in the above passage.

A3. In how many different ways may the word *judging* be parsed? Illustrate each of them by a sentence.

[45] *Examination Papers 1892*, Senior Students, UK: University of Cambridge Local Examinations Syndicate, 1892. © UCLES

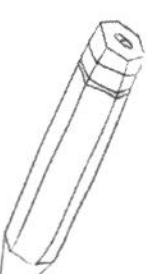

WRITE an essay on one of the following subjects:

(a) Technical Education.
(b) Gambling.
(c) An alarm of fire.
(d) "All that glisters is not gold."
(e) "To be prepared for war is one of the most effectual means of preserving peace."

A3. Standard gold consists of eleven parts by weight of pure gold to one part of alloy, and 40 lbs. Troy of standard gold is coined into 1869 sovereigns. Find (i) the weight of a sovereign in grains correct to three places of decimals, and (ii) the cost of the alloy required for one million of sovereigns, supposing it to consist of silver at 4s. per ounce Troy.

B4. On a certain day $2\frac{1}{2}$ per cent. Consols were at $96\frac{1}{4}$ and Egyptian 3 per cents. at $102\frac{1}{2}$. A man, who had a certain sum to invest, calculated that if he invested it in one of these stocks he would have a larger income by £5. 4s. than if he invested it in the other. What sum had he to invest?

Throughout the history of examinations in Singapore, UCLES had proven to be a reliable partner, even in the midst of tumultuous events and developments in the UK. During World War I (1914–1918) in Europe, business was as usual in UCLES. The *Sixty-First Annual Report of the Syndicate*, put up after the war, stated the following:

> It is however satisfactory to record that throughout the war all question papers have been duly transmitted to the Centres in time for the holding of examinations with the exception of a partial failure in Dec 1917 and that the candidates' answers have all been safely conveyed from Centres to Cambridge except for a small number of Higher Local answers which were on a ship torpedoed off the Indian coast in June 1917.[46]

During World War II (1939–1945), in the midst of Britain's involvement in a two-front war in Europe and the Far East, UCLES examinations

---

[46] It was not stated if answers from Singapore were amongst those which were on the torpedoed ship. *The Sixty-First Annual Report of the Syndicate, 21 May 1919*, UK: University of Cambridge Local Examinations Syndicate, 1919, p. 5.

continued in domestic and overseas centres. In 1939, there was a delay in the arrival of scripts in Cambridge from the different centres, and a consequent delay in the award and issue of results.[47] Examinations continued up to 1941, before the Japanese Occupation of Singapore. As part of the emergency arrangements arising from the war, UCLES proposed special considerations for the candidates, for the issue of 'certificates suitable for local acceptance, to candidates recommended by the Education Department on the basis of school records, if it should prove impossible to conduct the award based on marked scripts'.[48] Yet, in spite of the war, nearly all scripts arrived from centres in Malaya, and arrangements were made to publish the results of the 1941 examination.[49] In 1941, over 1,000 students took the Malayan (Cambridge) School Certificate Examinations in Singapore, and 700 passed.[50]

The Cambridge examinations had established and raised the standard of English stream education tremendously. The secondary school curriculum, based entirely on the Cambridge examinations, became the basis for entrance into Raffles College (established in 1928) and scholarships for further studies in the UK.

EXAMINATIONS IN VERNACULAR SCHOOLS

The British exercised varying degrees of control over vernacular schools. The only vernacular education that was consistently supported and provided free by the British government was for the Malay community, as the government saw 'the indigenous population and the vernacular' as Malay.[51]

Malay Stream Schools

In Singapore, the first recorded formal education in Malay was in the

---

[47] *The Eighty-Second Annual Report of the Syndicate, 2 May 1940*, UK: University of Cambridge Local Examinations Syndicate, 1940.

[48] *Syndicate Minutes*, 5 March 1942, Para 2(c), UK: University of Cambridge Local Examinations Syndicate.

[49] *The Eighty-Fourth Annual Report of the Syndicate, 4 June 1942*, UK: University of Cambridge Local Examinations Syndicate, 1942, p. 1.

[50] J. B. Neilson, *Annual Report of the Department of Education 1946*, Singapore: Government Printing Office, 1947, p. 1.

[51] Theodore R. Doraisamy (ed.), *150 Years of Education in Singapore*, Singapore: Stamford College Press Ltd, 1969, p. 23.

Singapore Free School in 1834.[52] Mr B. P. Keasberry of the London Missionary Society opened a school for the Malays in 1840, but it was short-lived.[53] He also opened a free boarding school in River Valley which continued until he passed away in 1875.[54] Subsequently, two vernacular schools, supported by the government, were established at Kampong Glam and Telok Blangah in 1856.[55] In 1872, A. M. Skinner, the Inspector of Schools, established Malay language schools based on the Koran classes. These schools provided instruction from Standards I to V. From 1892, 16 night schools were also opened in Singapore for Malays to learn reading and writing in their own language. The standards and examinations were similar to those of the government schools.[56]

Akin to the government and aided English schools, the Malay schools were also under the control of the Inspector of Schools, who would pay frequent visits to the schools and conduct annual examinations. The teachers would receive a small bonus based on the examination results.[57] In Singapore, any Malay boy who had passed Standard IV in a Malay school could receive free education in one of the government English schools.[58] In 1913, 264 Malay boys were eligible for free education in government English schools.[59] Malay students were encouraged to take Malay in the Cambridge examinations, as it was thought that Malay would be useful to the acquisition of the English language.[60]

The Malay stream schools thus had a systematic system of education and examinations, similar to that of the English schools, up to the primary level. In 1916, R. O. Winstedt was appointed as the Director of Education. A Malay scholar who was dedicated to the improvement of

<hr>

[52] Francis H. K. Wong & Y. H. Gwee, *Official Reports on Education: Straits Settlements and the Federated Malay States 1870–1939*, Singapore: Pan Pacific Book Distributors (S) Pte Ltd, 1980, Introduction, p. 2.

[53] J. B. Neilson, *Annual Report of the Department of Education 1946*, Singapore: Government Printing Office, 1947, p. 2.

[54] Ibid.

[55] Ibid.

[56] "Report of a Committee appointed to enquire into the system of vernacular education in the colony" in *Straits Settlements Paper laid before the Legislative Council*, No. 4, 2 Feb 1894, Singapore: National Archives of Singapore, p. 29.

[57] "Education of the Colony" *Straits Settlements Paper laid before the Legislative Council, 31 January 1913*, Singapore: National Archives of Singapore, p. 13.

[58] Ibid.

[59] Ibid.

[60] H. A. Wyndham, *Problems of Imperial Trusteeship. Native Education. Ceylon, Java, Formosa, the Philippines, French Indo-China, and British Malaya*, London: Oxford University Press, 1933, pp. 213–214.

Malay education, he extended English stream education to Malays 'who were able to profit by it'.[61] The annual examinations became the means by which Malay boys were selected for continuation in English stream schools. In 1919, Malay boys who had passed Standard III were admitted to English stream schools, on condition that they passed Standard IV in the Malay language subsequently.[62] In 1924, Special Malay classes were organised for Malay boys who were transferred from Malay to English schools, and who had completed Standard IV. After 2 years of attending the Special Malay classes to study English, these Malay boys were placed in Standard III or IV of the regular English schools.[63]

Up to 1941, higher education was limited to only the few privileged Malays as British policy was not inclined towards developing 'indigenous leadership to assume the duties of eventual self-government'.[64] Success in annual examinations was the means by which the few Malay boys gained access to English stream examinations.

Chinese Stream Schools

In Singapore, the earliest record of Chinese stream schools was made in 1829, of two Cantonese schools at Kampong Glam and Pekin Street and a Fujian (Hokkien) school in Pekin Street.[65] The early schools imparted a classical education that was of little relevance to the needs of the Straits Settlements.[66] In the 19th century, the British government adopted a neutral attitude towards Chinese stream schools. These schools were left very much to the Chinese community, largely funded by groups of Chinese merchants or individual wealthy members of the community.[67] The government only provided financial assistance to Chinese stream

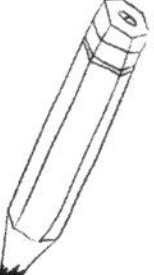

---

[61] Theodore R. Doraisamy (ed.), *150 Years of Education in Singapore*, Singapore: Stamford College Press Ltd, 1969, p. 107.

[62] Ibid., pp. 107–108.

[63] Ibid., p. 108.

[64] Ibid., p. 109.

[65] Francis H. K. Wong & Y. H. Gwee, *Perspectives: The Development of Education in Malaysia and Singapore*, Kuala Lumpur, Singapore, Hong Kong: Heinmann Educational Books (Asia) Ltd, 1972, p. 3.

[66] Ibid.

[67] H. E. Wilson, *Social Engineering in Singapore: Educational Policies and Social Change 1819–1972*, Singapore: Singapore University Press, 1978, p. 24.

schools run by Christian missionaries and 'Free Schools' which conducted Chinese classes.[68]

From 1900 to 1919, the Chinese stream schools multiplied rapidly, with an orientation towards China and Chinese nationalism.[69] The structure of Chinese schools also followed the system in China: six years of primary school, three years of junior middle school and three years of senior middle school (6-3-3 system).[70]

Chinese stream education became politicised when the Chinese in Singapore hosted exiled reformers and revolutionaries from China, and were involved in the planning of several Chinese uprisings in 1907 and 1908.[71] Alarmed by this, the British government decided to exert some control over Chinese schools. In 1920, the colonial government required schools, teachers and managers to be registered. The government also had the power to make and enforce regulations relating to the conduct of schools and to declare schools unlawful where teaching was found to be revolutionary or in conflict with the interests of the government.[72] Another government measure was to provide grants-in-aid to Chinese stream schools which would require them to present its pupils for annual inspections and examinations. In 1935, the British government conducted annual common examinations for students in the 6th year of primary and 3rd year (Junior Middle III) of secondary schools.[73] These common examinations had been initiated in 1931 by the Hokkien Huay Kuan (Fujian Association) of Singapore to raise the standard amongst the Chinese stream schools. In 1939, the British administration set up a committee to design a curriculum based on the Malayan context, for Chinese stream primary schools.[74] These and subsequent attempts to

---

[68] Theodore R. Doraisamy (ed.), *150 Years of Education in Singapore*, Singapore: Stamford College Press Ltd, 1969, p. 29.

[69] Francis H. K. Wong & Y. H. Gwee, *Perspectives: The Development of Education in Malaysia and Singapore*, Kuala Lumpur, Singapore, Hong Kong: Heinmann Educational Books (Asia) Ltd, 1972, p. 8.

[70] Paul M. F. Chang, *Educational Development in a Plural Society: A Malaysian Case Study*, Singapore: Academia Publications, c. 1973, p. 19.

[71] S. Gopinathan, "Education" in Ernest C. T. Chew & Edwin Lee (eds), *A History of Singapore*, Singapore: Oxford University Press Pte Ltd, 1991, p. 270.

[72] Theodore R. Doraisamy (ed.), *150 Years of Education in Singapore*, Singapore: Stamford College Press Ltd, 1969, p. 87.

[73] L. E. Tan, *The Politics of Chinese Education in Malaya 1945–1961*, New York: Oxford University Press, 1997, p. 23.

[74] Ibid.

regulate Chinese stream schools were to lead to uncertainty and distrust by the Chinese community towards government efforts to restructure the system in the post-war period.[75]

The most obvious disparity between Chinese stream schools and English stream schools would be that the former did not yield recognised qualifications for employment. The Standard IV, VII and Cambridge Certificates from English stream schools were far more attractive for employment than the Chinese stream school-leaving certificates. In the post-war period, these frustrated pupils of the Chinese stream schools would later become easy targets for the communists.[76]

Tamil Stream Schools

In Singapore, the first recorded formal education in Tamil was in Singapore Free School in 1834.[77] Some Christian missionary organisations also supported the Tamil stream schools. In 1873, Tamil education was revived due to the demand for Tamil interpreters and English-speaking Indian clerks. In 1873 and 1876, two Anglo-Tamil schools were established for the first time for the learning of the English language through the Tamil medium and were conducted by school-masters from Ceylon.[78] However, these two schools which were to be 'Branch English schools' to the Raffles Institution had less than 5% of the pupils who continued schooling until Standard VI.[79] According to Doraisamy, 'around the turn of the century Tamil education in Singapore was again non-existent in government-aided schools'.[80] Notwithstanding, the Education Codes of 1908 and 1914 suggested a curriculum for Standard I to V for Tamil vernacular schools that received grants-in-aid.[81] Due to the small population of Indians, there were not

[75] H. E. Wilson, *Social Engineering in Singapore: Educational Policies and Social Change 1819–1972*, Singapore: Singapore University Press, 1978, p. 63.
[76] Paul M. F. Chang, *Educational Development in a Plural Society: A Malaysian Case Study*, Singapore: Academia Publications, c. 1973, p. 19.
[77] Francis H. K. Wong & Y. H. Gwee, *Perspectives: The Development of Education in Malaysia and Singapore*, Kuala Lumpur, Singapore, Hong Kong: Heinmann Educational Books (Asia) Ltd, 1972, p. 9.
[78] Theodore R. Doraisamy (ed.), *150 Years of Education in Singapore*, Singapore: Stamford College Press Ltd, 1969, p. 117.
[79] Ibid.
[80] Ibid.
[81] *Revised Education Code for the Straits Settlements and Federated Malay States, 1908*, Appendix E, pp.128–130, and *Education Code for the Straits Settlements, 1914*, Appendix E, Singapore: National Archives of Singapore, pp. 21–22.

many separate Tamil vernacular schools.[82] In fact, the numbers of Indian students in English stream schools had always been more than that in Tamil stream schools.[83] Up to 1941, there were no government Tamil schools, and only about 1,000 pupils in 18 Tamil grant-in-aid schools.[84] It could be concluded that, apart from school-based examinations, the examinations in Tamil grant-in-aid schools were as prescribed by the education codes for annual examinations in Standard IV.

CONCLUSION

Education and examinations during early British colonial rule had inadvertently produced divisive tendencies due to, firstly, the plural nature of society; and secondly, the educational policies of the British, favouring English over vernacular education in Malay, Chinese and Tamil. In the words of historian H. E. Wilson, there was a 'fundamental inequality of treatment and opportunity which resulted from the absence of a single, clearly enunciated, guiding policy'.[85] Government attention and funding were monopolised by government and aided English stream schools.[86]

The educational divide was institutionalised by a system of examinations, subscribed by an emerging social class — the English educated. The English stream examinations, in particular the Cambridge examinations, had ensured opportunities for employment, producing a privileged class, segregated from the rest of society. In 1941, when the Pacific War broke out in the Far East and British rule in Singapore gave way to Japanese imperialism, there was still no common Malayan or Singaporean identity.

[82] Francis H. K. Wong & Y. H. Gwee, *Perspectives: The Development of Education in Malaysia and Singapore*, Kuala Lumpur, Singapore, Hong Kong: Heinmann Educational Books (Asia) Ltd, 1972, p. 10.

[83] J. B. Neilson, *Annual Report of the Department of Education 1946*, Singapore: Government Printing Office, 1947, p. 16.

[84] Theodore R. Doraisamy (ed.), *150 Years of Education in Singapore*, Singapore: Stamford College Press Ltd, 1969, p. 118.

[85] H. E. Wilson, *Social Engineering in Singapore: Educational Policies and Social Change 1819–1972*, Singapore: Singapore University Press, 1978, p. 29.

[86] Ibid., p. 52.

CHAPTER

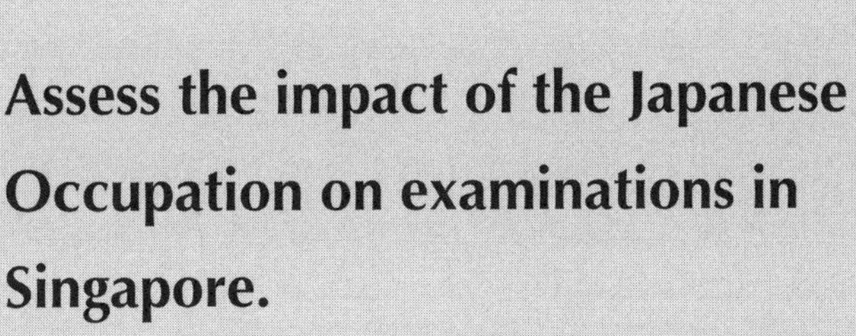
Assess the impact of the Japanese Occupation on examinations in Singapore.

The Pacific War broke out on 7 December 1941, and by the following day, Japanese warplanes were raining bombs on Singapore. Arthur Alexander Thompson, who was about 17 years of age recalled:

I was...in the Senior Cambridge Examination, that's my final. And the exams had commenced.... I was in the Victoria Institution.... What happened was this...early hours of Monday morning, Singapore is bombed with first raid of Japanese bombers. And when I went to school.... Our examination hall was upstairs. So we went up, teacher says, "war has broken out", and told us what we were to do when the siren comes on. We were doing our history of the British Empire. And when the siren goes, all you do is cover your papers, examination papers, turned it over and get under the desk.[1]

December 1941 turned out to be the last year in which students like Arthur Alexander Thompson formally sat for the Cambridge School Certificate, before Singapore fell to the Japanese on 15 February 1942. Notwithstanding the war, the University of Cambridge Local Examinations Syndicate (UCLES) continued to offer the Cambridge examinations to its overseas centres.

[1] *Oral History Interview with A. A. Thompson, Accession No. 143,* Singapore: National Archives of Singapore.

For three and a half years, Singapore found itself under the administration of another imperial power. The seizure of Singapore had been carried out as part of an overall plan to break Western domination of Southeast Asia and to replace it with Japanese domination. Education was recognised as the most powerful instrument to obliterate Western influences, 'unite the cultures of individual nationalities' and 'promote a sense of brotherhood of all Asians living in Japanese conquered territories'.[2] To this end, the immediate impact of the Japanese Occupation was the institution of a Japanese education system and a different form of examinations in Singapore. Japanese-language proficiency examinations and technical examinations replaced the Cambridge examinations as the mainstay of examinations in Singapore.

A DIFFERENT COLONIAL MASTER, A DIFFERENT EDUCATION SYSTEM

Like the British government, the Japanese did not establish a single school system in Singapore. In the immediate aftermath of invasion, schools were destroyed, closed or looted. In April 1942, the Japanese hastily reopened the primary schools. Through the *Syonan Times* (the English language newspaper which replaced *The Straits Times*), children up to the age of 14 were asked to register for schools.[3] Education was entrusted to the municipality consisting of a Japanese director and a small staff. Mamoru Shinozaki, the former press attaché on the staff of the Japanese consulate in Singapore, was made the Chief Officer of Education. Shinozaki's primary goal was to take the children off the street. However, the Japanese, in their haste to re-open schools, allowed the pre-war system of education to re-emerge.[4] The old system, with its English, Chinese, Malay and Tamil stream schools, to some extent, was revived.

The former English stream schools became 'Public Schools' and were re-named in accordance with the streets on which they were located.

---

[2] H. E. Wilson, *Social Engineering in Singapore: Educational Policies and Social Change 1819–1972*, Singapore: Singapore University Press, 1978, p. 85.

[3] *Syonan Times*, 25 March 2602 (1942).

[4] H. E. Wilson, *Social Engineering in Singapore: Educational Policies and Social Change 1819–1972*, Singapore: Singapore University Press, 1978, pp. 7–8.

For example, Raffles Institution became Beach Road Boys' School and Singapore Chinese Girls' School became the Emerald Hill Girls' School, although the secondary schools were never re-opened. The official policy forbade the teaching of English as a subject. However, English could be used if Malay or Chinese failed to be understood. In practice, English continued to be used to a greater or lesser extent in schools, and was often taught surreptitiously.[5] The Japanese, however, did not forbid the use of the vernacular languages in the schools. In the Malay stream schools, the use and teaching of Malay was permitted. The few Tamil stream schools which re-opened were mainly advocating nationalist propaganda for India's independence movement. The Chinese stream schools were permitted to teach Chinese as a subject. In practice, all subjects were taught in Chinese. Some schools took advantage of the fact that Chinese was the last lesson of the morning to lengthen the time for that subject.[6]

The Japanese administration did impose some extent of uniformity on the schools, via the compulsory teaching and learning of the Japanese language (Nippon-Go). Japanese replaced English as the language of administration, government and communication, and became the key instrument to wipe out Western influences in order to 'save Asians from continuing to be the victims of the English'[7] and impart Japanese cultural values and attitudes. Japanese language lessons formed the mainstay of the curriculum. The general school curriculum included Japanese songs, Japanese reading, writing and propaganda, some arithmetic and nature study. In the morning, the students sang the Japanese national anthem and bowed in a north-easterly direction to the emperor in Tokyo. Local teachers were required to learn Japanese and even take examinations; as such they were often 'only a few steps ahead of their pupils in their knowledge of Japanese'.[8] Japanese teachers were also hired to teach in these schools. In addition, the Japanese installed radio receivers in 87 elementary schools to transmit daily lessons and inaugurated 'the

[5] J. B. Neilson, *Annual Report of the Department of Education 1946*, Singapore: Government Printing Office, 1947, p. 2.
[6] Ibid., p. 3.
[7] *Syonan Times*, 28 February, 2602 (1942).
[8] Ibid., p. 4.

first regular schools broadcasting service in the island'.[9] In general, however, there was low enthusiasm for the curriculum. Enrolment declined drastically during the war years.[10] Chinese parents in particular were reluctant to send their children to schools for fear that the latter would be conscripted into the Japanese army. In addition, there was a shortage of Japanese textbooks and equipment. Mr Soh Chuan Lam, who attended a private school, remembered that his Japanese teacher had to write the textbook himself and get it printed for the students.[11]

The zeal to spread the Japanese language led to the setting up of numerous Japanese language schools, a well-known one being the Japanese Military Administration National Language School at Queen Street, later renamed as the Queen Street Japanese Language School. These language schools were initially run by the Japanese army and placed under the Propaganda Department before being brought under the Municipality Education Department. There were elementary, intermediate, advanced and research stages for the language schools. Students were taught to read, write and speak Japanese by former teachers from the Japanese schools. Each lesson was 'two hours and it was twice a week…language,…singing lessons, physical education and fortnightly there was some sort of lessons on culture and all that'.[12] There were also private language schools such as the Syonan Honganji, housed in a temple and run by a priest. Mr Soh, who studied there, believed that the ashes of the Japanese soldiers were kept at the temple.[13]

---

[9] H. E. Wilson, *Social Engineering in Singapore: Educational Policies and Social Change 1819–1972*, Singapore: Singapore University Press, 1978, p. 85.

[10] In 1941, the number of registered schools was 448: 31 Government and Aided schools, 20 Malay schools, 370 Chinese schools and 18 Tamil schools. This declined to 124 registered schools at the end of 1945: 37 English schools, 21 Malay schools and 66 Chinese schools. In J. B. Neilson, *Annual Report of the Department of Education 1946*, Singapore: Government Printing Office, 1947, pp. 1 & 5.

[11] *Oral History Interview with Soh Chuan Lam, Accession No. 304*, Singapore: National Archives of Singapore, p. 28.

[12] Ibid., p. 38.

[13] Ibid., p. 31.

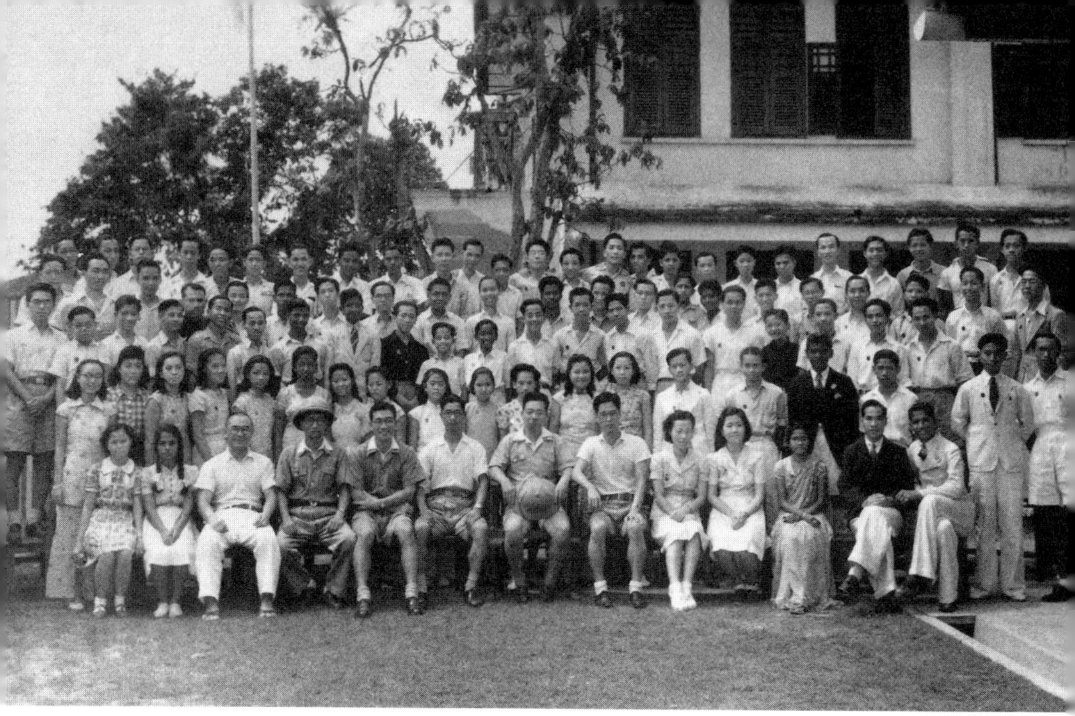

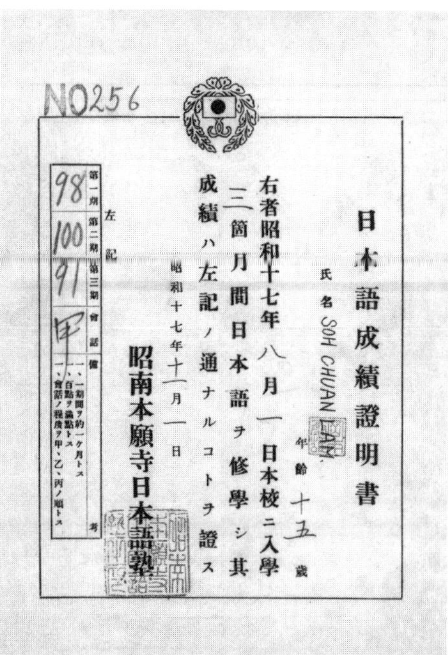

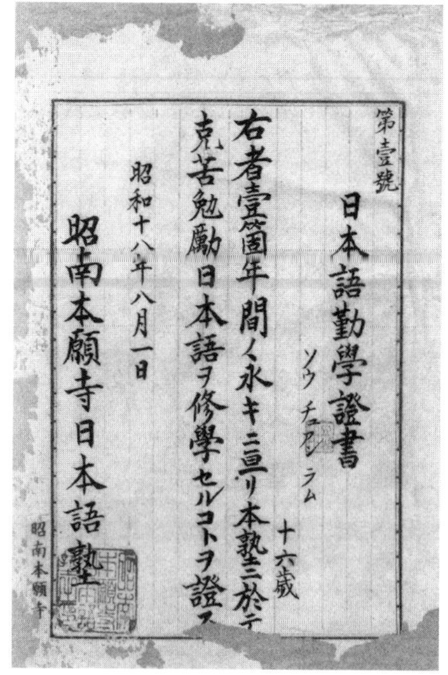

Certificates from Syonan Honganji. (Mr Soh Chuan Lam, Courtesy of National Archives of Singapore)

JAPANESE LANGUAGE PROFICIENCY EXAMINATIONS

The Japanese introduced the Japanese Language Proficiency Examinations for elementary school boys as well as those over 15 years of age. The *Syonan Times* indicated that these proficiency examinations would be conducted once every six months and historian Lee Geok Boi believed they were held right up to the end of the Occupation.[14]

The different grades of Japanese examinations were elementary, intermediate and advanced. Candidates were required to pass the following tests:[15]

Elementary Grade:	Oral test in plain Nippon Language, Katakana writing.
Middle Grade:	Easy Kanji reading (150 words); Katakana and Hiragana writing.
Higher Grade:	Easy Kanji reading (360 words); Easy Kanji writing; Katakana and Hiragana writing.

Mr Soh, a candidate of the examination, recalled that for the oral examination, they had to speak in front of three Japanese teachers, 'and they asked questions and so on…the oral examiners, they were quite friendly'.[16] On the grading of these examinations, Mr Soh mentioned that a special grade was added later and he recalled, 'so, being quite good in the Japanese knowledge, I took the highest one…. I passed that one, the whole of Singapore only 32 passed this examination… considered the highest examination'.[17]

Students who passed the Japanese Language Proficiency Examinations were given certificates and promoted to the next grade. Like the Cambridge certificates, the Japanese-issued certificates had economic value. They were recognised by the Japanese companies, and for those who passed, 'they would be paid an extra allowance of $50 a month'.[18]

[14] G. B. Lee, *The Syonan Years: Singapore under Japanese Rule 1942–1945*, Singapore: National Archives of Singapore and Epigram Pte Ltd, 2005, p. 171.

[15] *Syonan Times*, 15 March 2603 (1943).

[16] *Oral History Interview with Soh Chuan Lam, Accession No. 304*, Singapore: National Archives of Singapore, p. 74.

[17] Ibid., p. 72.

[18] Ibid., p. 76.

In fact, the Japanese constantly reminded the people that they 'will be at a disadvantage in applying for any position without a knowledge of Nippon-Go' and not to waste their time.[19] To encourage the people, the Japanese gave out round metal badges to candidates who passed the proficiency examinations, to show that they could speak the Japanese language. On these badges were inscribed 'Nippon-Go' and the grade obtained by the candidates. In addition, to show 'profound admiration' of the language proficiency of the students, the Japanese officials and members of the Japanese press held a roundtable conference, 'at which only Nippon-Go was spoken'. This was for students who passed with honours at the first highest grade examination held.[20]

To sum up, the Japanese, through the sustained propagation and examination of the Japanese language, sought to promote the cultural affinity of the Japanese with the diverse racial groups and the essential sense of Asian brotherhood. This was not unlike the British government who also took deliberate steps to promote English as the medium of instruction. In both cases, education and the medium of instruction served to further imperial control of the colony. One key difference was that the Japanese had a systematic policy promoting the Japanese language, whereas the British did not impose a mandatory and uniform policy of English teaching and testing on the vernacular schools. In this sense, though both imperial powers did not establish a national education system, the Japanese educational policy saw greater uniformity resulting from the zealous promotion and testing of its language. As historian H. E. Wilson summed it up, 'the ideal of a single type of school providing a common educational experience for the children of the major communities and equipping the pupils with a lingua franca was clearly intended.'[21] The Japanese, however, ultimately failed to establish their language as the lingua franca of Singapore given the short period of occupation. The English language, not made the mandatory medium of instruction and examination for all school students by the British, ironically took root as the lingua franca of post-independent Singapore.

---

[19] Quoted in H. E. Wilson, *Social Engineering in Singapore: Educational Policies and Social Change 1819–1972*, Singapore: Singapore University Press, 1978, p. 103.
[20] *Syonan Shinbum*, 6 June 2605 (1945).
[21] H. E. Wilson, *Social Engineering in Singapore: Educational Policies and Social Change 1819–1972*, Singapore: Singapore University Press, 1978, p. 93.

TECHNICAL EXAMINATIONS

Technical education was provided by the Japanese to meet the needs of their military. Mechanical and engineering skills were promoted. In place of secondary education were a number of centres for the teaching of vocational and technical skills. These technical schools catered to boys aged 14 and above. The students were required to pay a very small stipend, but food and lodging were provided and the course was free.[22] Most of the lessons were practical as the students could not write. So for examinations, Mr Victor Krusemann, an instructor at an aircraft mechanics school in Changi, recalled, 'We just had to check them verbally. We used to put all the parts on the table, and ask them "Bring a carburettor to me…" in Japanese we tell them. They will point out. That's good enough.'[23] Certificates were awarded to graduates of technical schools. These schools, however, suffered from a lack of equipment. The Education Department in fact had to appeal to the army for some of the equipment. This limitation aside, historian H. E. Wilson believed that 'the proliferation of technical schools and trade schools produced the nucleus of the skilled labour force that was to play an important role in the metamorphosis of post-war Singapore'.[24] But to a British internee at Changi Prison Camp, these centres were '….merely cloaks for enforcing child labour'.[25]

CONCLUSION

In retrospect, during the Japanese Occupation period, the examinations were mainly focused on narrow testing on Japanese language competency and technical skills. During the British period, the examinations had ranged from annual examinations in the primary schools to the Cambridge Local Examinations in the secondary schools, as well as vernacular examinations organised by Chinese, Malay and Indian schools. There was a range

---

[22] G. B. Lee, *The Syonan Years: Singapore under Japanese Rule 1942–1945*, Singapore: National Archives of Singapore and Epigram Pte Ltd, 2005, p. 185.

[23] *Oral History Interview with Victor Krusemann, Accession No. 375,* Singapore: National Archives of Singapore, p. 140.

[24] H. E. Wilson, *Social Engineering in Singapore: Educational Policies and Social Change 1819–1972*, Singapore: Singapore University Press, 1978, p. 20.

[25] H. R. Cheeseman, *A Brief Review of the Educational Programme in the Singapore Internment Camp* [Changi Prison until 1944 and then Sime Road Camp], UK: University of Cambridge Local Examinations Syndicate, 2 September 1945, p. 5.

of subjects examined, from academic subjects in English schools and Chinese classical studies to subjects like basket-weaving.

Notwithstanding, examinations continued to serve a utilitarian purpose for both the political administration and examination candidates. The Japanese administration used the language proficiency and technical examinations to promote its political and socio-economic agenda. In turn, candidates with Japanese language certificates had better job prospects and could obtain higher allowance from Japanese companies while vocational and technical school graduates could find ready employment in the industries. In the same way, the British government had used annual examinations as a means to exert some form of control over the plural school system, and to raise the quality of education. In turn, successful School Certificate candidates from English schools could aspire for scholarships such as the Queen's Scholarship to further their studies in the United Kingdom or apply for jobs in the British administration.

From a short-term standpoint, a Japanese system appeared to have swiftly supplanted the British system of education and examinations. Notwithstanding that, a tenuous link with education in the pre-war British past survived in the Sime Road Camp during this period, thus forging continuity between the pre- and post-war periods (see Chapter 3). From the present-day vantage point, Japanese education and examinations were ephemeral — their impact barely extended beyond that of the Japanese Occupation period.

CHAPTER

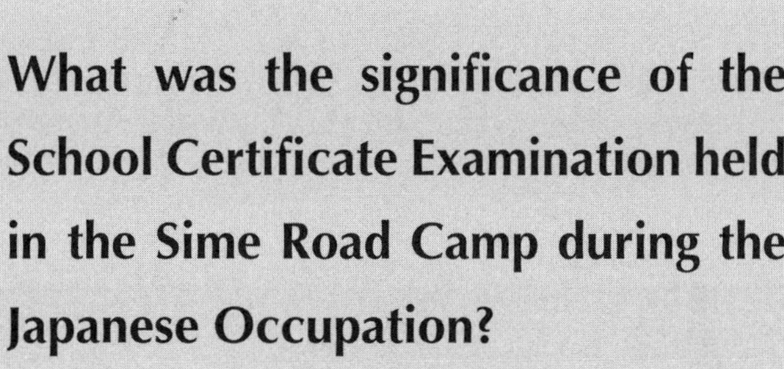

What was the significance of the School Certificate Examination held in the Sime Road Camp during the Japanese Occupation?

The question papers were typed under conditions of secrecy and each set of question papers was placed in a sealed envelope which was opened in the presence of the candidates five minutes before the time fixed for the beginning of the paper.[1]

H. R. Cheeseman
Report on Sime Road Certificate Examination,
20 February 1945

Unknown to the Japanese and many Singaporeans, at one particular prison camp in Sime Road, the pre-war Cambridge Examinations persevered, albeit on a very small scale and involving a mere handful of candidates. Its continuation must be credited to the vision of H. R. Cheeseman, the Camp Education Officer at Changi Prison, and a group of brave internees who were mostly once members of the Malayan Education Service. As the Japanese defeat closed in, Cheeseman wrote *A Brief Review of the Educational Programme in the Singapore Internment Camp* based largely on memory as there was considerable risk in keeping records then. This account obtained from the Cambridge Assessment Archives gave a fascinating glimpse into the Cambridge Examination conducted in an internment camp.

EDUCATION AT CHANGI PRISON

In the first few days of internment at Changi, the Japanese sent for Cheeseman and made him personally responsible for the education of the boys under 16. Cheeseman had served as the Deputy Director of

---

[1] H. R. Cheeseman, *Report on Sime Road Certificate Examination*, UK: University of Cambridge Local Examinations Syndicate, 20 February 1945.

Education, Malaya and Examinations Secretary. He was to become the Camp Education Officer for the whole period of internment. He was also the Group Representative for four prison huts, Deputy Commander of the Central (Administrative) area of the Sime Road Camp, and Chairman of the Camp Leisure Hours Committee. Camp education came under the direction of the Leisure Hours Committee.[2]

Up to 10 October 1943, the educational programme for the men and boys at Changi Prison was extensive. Fatigues were not excessive and there were some 2,000 students in the classes, with internees paying for textbooks, exercise books and other equipment from their own funds–expended for by their sympathizers outside the prison. The adult internees were taught in the open air, with the students seated on the grounds or improvised chairs. They were taught in an 'amazing' number of subjects by internees who had been teachers before the war. The Camp School for the boys proved less easy to arrange because of the difficulty in getting instructors who had to teach on top of performing prison fatigue. In the end, the task was taken up mainly by a group of older adult internees. There was close linkage between education provided in the men's and women's camps. The Japanese accepted Cheeseman as the Advisor to the women's camp and permitted the Headmistress, Mrs B. L. Milne of the Johore Education Department, to hold periodic discussions with him. The special syllabus drawn up for the men's camp was followed as far as possible by the women's camp.

This prison educational programme came to an abrupt halt when the Japanese army descended on the camp on 10 October 1943. They suspected the prisoners of masterminding a sabotage on Japanese tankers at the Singapore Harbour. More than 50 prisoners were interrogated and tortured, and 15 died as a result. The Camp School was closed, most textbooks and notebooks were removed, and all teaching was forbidden. Nevertheless Cheeseman and some adult internees did not give up; 'as much as possible was done surreptitiously for the boys who were taken individually in sequestered corners of the Prison'.[3] This

[2] H. R. Cheeseman, A *Brief Review of the Educational Programme in the Singapore Internment Camp*, UK: University of Cambridge Local Examinations Syndicate, 2 September 1945, p. 1.
[3] Ibid., p. 2.

clandestine tutoring of individuals, done at great risk to the teachers, continued after the transfer to Sime Road Camp in May 1944.

Sime Road Camp Cambridge Examination

Sime Road Camp, located at the junction of Adam Road and Sime Road, comprised a collection of huts. On 1 May 1944, all the civilian prisoners, about 3,500, including Cheeseman, were transferred to Sime Road Camp. It was at this camp that the School Certificate Examination was conducted, following the scheme to be used if question papers were lost in the midst of war in Europe. In July 1944, the Japanese agreed to re-open the school. Boys under 15 were organised into Lower School and boys above 15 went to the Upper School. The Lower School boys were either instructed at the prison church or the school dormitory and under trees. The Upper School boys met their instructors in any available shady spot and the largest group consisted of three boys. Teaching the boys at Sime Road Camp proved more demanding as the open nature of the Camp limited the shade available for conducting classes, unlike the enclosed Changi Prison. At the end of the internment, there was an enrolment of 105 Lower and 11 Upper School boys. There were far fewer Upper School boys as the Japanese had ordered the older boys to do some three to six hours of fatigue a day, leaving them too exhausted for instruction, whereas the Lower School boys were permitted to do two hours of classes, thus making it possible to continue Lower School classes. The higher number of younger boys was also due to an influx of new internees — mainly domiciled Eurasians and Jews — to the Camp.

Despite wartime deprivation and hardship, Cheeseman had a vision for the boys' future:

> I drew up a long-term programme in Changi and decided early that the Upper School boys who made the necessary progress should take the School Certificate Examination in December 1944...I felt that it would be an advantage to have an objective... I did not think for a moment that we should still be in internment in December 1944.[4]

[4] Ibid., p. 3.

Cheeseman thus went about organising the Cambridge School Certificate Examination for a small group of candidates. The first examination took place from 15 to 27 January 1945 (excluding Sunday, 21 January), and a second one was arranged for special candidates in August 1945 and 'completed on the very day preceding that in which we got news of Japan's surrender'.[5] The subjects taken were English (English Composition, English Language and Oral English), English Literature, Elementary Mathematics, English History, Geography, French and Dutch. It appeared from the archival records that seven candidates were presented for the January examination, sitting a range of subjects while one Russian boy sat for English. In the August examination, it appeared that there were three candidates.[6] The women's camp presented two girls for the examination.[7]

The arrangements of the Cambridge Examination for a mere handful of candidates involved an immense amount of labour. Special care was taken to conform to what was believed to be standards of the University of Cambridge Local Examinations Syndicate (UCLES). There were two examination centres, one for the boys and one for the girls. As the regulations for the School Certificate Examination were not available in the Camp, a syllabus was drawn up, and the requirements of the examination (including details of the question papers in terms of the time allotted, the number and choice of questions, and rubrics for each paper) were compiled with the assistance of those who had been teachers before the war. The question papers were typed under conditions of secrecy and each set of question papers was placed in a sealed envelope which was opened in the presence of the candidates five minutes before the start time of the question papers. Candidates were told 'to write on both sides of the paper and it was necessary to use paper varying in size and quality'.[8] With reference to the two girls from the women's camp presented for examination, Cheeseman related, 'it

---

[5] Ibid.

[6] *Schedule of entries*, January 1945 and *Schedule of results*, August 1945, UK: University of Cambridge Local Examinations Syndicate.

[7] H. R. Cheeseman, A *Brief Review of the Educational Programme in the Singapore Internment Camp*, UK: University of Cambridge Local Examinations Syndicate, 2 September 1945, p. 4.

[8] *Sime Road School Certificate Examination*, UK: University of Cambridge Local Examinations Syndicate, p. 1.

was arranged for the question papers to be smuggled over there and the scripts smuggled back to me'.[9]

To ensure comparability of examination conditions and marking standards of the two examinations, Miss C. E. Renton served as the presiding examiner for the girls while Cheeseman presided over the boys. Cheeseman also acted as the moderator for the examinations as a whole. In marking too, Cheeseman sought to adhere strictly in accordance with what was believed as the syndicate's requirements. None of the examiners selected had taught any of the candidates. For each subject, there were two examiners who jointly set the paper and jointly marked the scripts. The scheme of marking was as follows:[10]

A	Very Good	75% upwards
G	Good	61 – 74%
C	Pass with Credit	51 – 60%
P	Pass	41 – 50%
W	Weak Pass	33⅓ – 40%
F	Failure	26 up to 33⅓%
B	Bad Failure	25% and less

The grades awarded were Grades I, II and III, and F (Failure). Below is a copy of the schedule of results for the examination in January 1945, containing details of subjects sat for, and the grades obtained.

---

[9] H. R. Cheeseman, A *Brief Review of the Educational Programme in the Singapore Internment Camp,* UK: University of Cambridge Local Examinations Syndicate, 2 September 1945, p. 4.

[10] *Sime Road School Certificate Examination,* UK: University of Cambridge Local Examinations Syndicate, p. 1.

Regd. No. ....

Date	Offence	Reported by

5

Sime Road Camp
School Certificate Examination
January 1945

Results in the Whole Examination

- I = Grade I
- II = Grade II
- III = Grade III
- F = Failure

120   Exam in Full

Results in Whole Examination	English	Composition	Language	Oral English	English Literature	History	Geography	Religious Knowledge	Gospels	Acts of the Apostles	French	Dutch	Elementary Mathematics	Arithmetic	Algebra	Geometry	Hygiene with Physiology	Shorthand
III⁴	p⁶	p⁷	p⁴	c⁷	-	-	-	p²	w¹	c²	g³	-	p⁴	w²	w⁴	p⁴	p⁶	-
III³	w⁸	w⁸	F	g⁴	p⁷	-	c¹	-	-	-	d¹	-	c¹	p¹	p²	d¹	c²	-
F	p⁷	p⁵	w⁷	g⁴	c⁴ (Eng)	F	-	-	-	-	g⁵	-	F	w⁵	b	w⁵	c²	-
F	c²	g³	c³	g⁴	g² (Eng)	p	-	-	-	-	d²	-	b	b	b	w⁵	c¹	-
II²	c³	g²	p⁶	g¹	p⁵	-	p²	p²	-	-	g⁴	c	p²	w³	p¹	g³	-	-
F	c⁵	c⁴	p⁵	g¹	p⁶ (BE)	F	-	-	w³	w³	w⁷	-	b	b	b	b	c⁴	-
II¹	g¹	g¹	c²	g¹	a¹ (BE)	c	-	p¹	w¹	g¹	c⁶	-	p³	w³	w³	g²	c⁵	F
Pass with Credit	c⁴	b⁶	g¹	c³	c³													

Eng = English History
BE = History of British Empire

Subject Marks:

- b = Bad Failure
- F̄ = Failure
- w = Weak Pass
- p = Pass
- c = Pass with Credit
- g = Good
- d = Very Good

H.R. Cheeseman
Examinations Secretary
20.2.1945

Sime Road Camp School Certificate Examination Results January 1945 © UCLES[11]

[11] *Results in the whole examination*, January 1945, UK: University of Cambridge Local Examinations Syndicate.

When the candidates were informed of their results, they were told that application would be made for the examinations to be accepted by the Malayan Government and UCLES, but that no assurance could be given that the examinations would be accepted. In his report to UCLES, Cheeseman highlighted the 'disabilities' faced by the candidates and their teachers in preparing for the examination, with the chief disability being 'undoubtedly the low mental condition of instructors and candidates, owing mainly to diet and environment, though there were also other unavoidable handicaps of captivity'.[12]

At the Oversea Committee Preliminary Meeting held after the war on 2 November 1945, UCLES considered the recommendations made by examiners who had seen the scripts and members of the Awarding Committee. The syndicate agreed to recognise the Sime Road Camp Examination and decided to issue a school certificate mentioning the special circumstances under which the examinations took place[13] which 'reflect the credit of all concerned'.[14] With the school certificate, the few boys and girls who braved prison conditions to sit the examination had a ray of hope for their future in the post-war period, as the British returned as rulers and the certification was recognised. In contrast, the Japanese examination certificates and badges issued to candidates outside the prison were of little use once the Japanese surrendered.

The Sime Road Camp Examination was significant in that it marked a continuity of the Cambridge examinations, which were reinstated in the immediate post-war period. It attested to the resilience of the British examination system that had made its imprint in Singapore half a century before the Japanese Occupation — conditions of examinations, confidentiality of question papers, impartiality of examiners, comparability of marking standards, awarding of grades and certification were in accordance with the Cambridge tradition, albeit in the clandestine context of war. The commitment of individuals such as Cheeseman, his predecessors and successors to the cause of education played no small part in the continual development of education in Singapore.

[12] *Sime Road School Certificate Examination*, UK: University of Cambridge Local Examinations Syndicate, p.1.

[13] *Overseas Committee Preliminary Meeting*, 2 Nov 1945, UK: University of Cambridge Local Examinations Syndicate.

[14] *The Eighty-Eighth Annual Report of the Syndicate*, 13 June 1946, UK: University of Cambridge Local Examinations Syndicate, 1946.

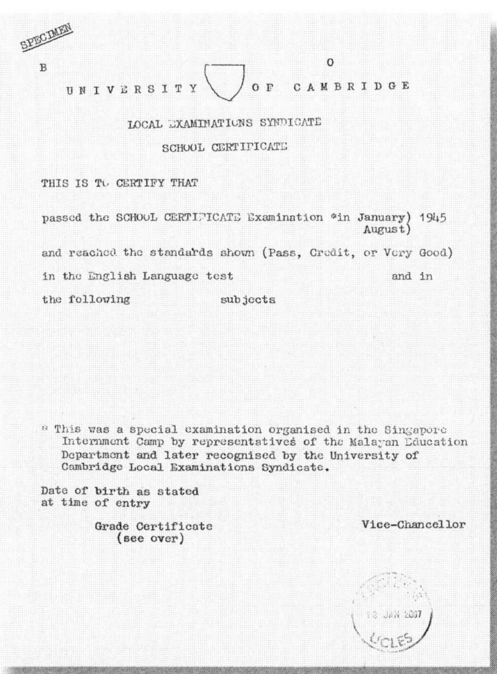

Sime Road Camp School Certificate © UCLES[15]

Sime Road Camp — Singapore, 1944–1945 (Lilian Gladys Tompkins 1893–1984 Reference Number C-095-027, Courtesy of the Alexander Turnbull Library, Wellington, New Zealand)

[15] *Sime Road Camp School Certificate*, UK: University of Cambridge Local Examinations Syndicate.

Ex-Prisoners-of-War doing their work at the Sime Road Camp. (Alex Glendinning, Courtesy of the National Archives of Singapore)

A Group of the Civilian Prisoners-of-War posing for a photo at the Sime Road Camp. (Alex Glendinning, Courtesy of the National Archives of Singapore)

B

The Post-War Years

(1946–1970s)

CHAPTER

Assess the development of education and examinations from the end of the Japanese Occupation to the attainment of self-government in Singapore.

‘ . . . the actual conditions of work and standards of education that could be provided in 1946 were still of necessity much below the pre-war level. Rehabilitation has still a long way to go – an important consideration in future planning and rate of advance.[1]

__J. B. Neilson__
Director of Education,
Colony of Singapore

The end of the Japanese Occupation saw the immediate rehabilitation of the pre-war British order, as well as a reorientation of education policy in view of the eventual self-government of the British colonies.

In the pre-war period, the British colonial government did not subscribe to the principle of equal opportunity in education for all children. Instead, the pre-war educational policy was ad-hoc and unequal in treatment, with free elementary education for Malays, more expenditure on English stream education, some grants in aid for Chinese stream schools, and a general neglect of Tamil stream education.

This attitude was to change, albeit only in principle, in the post-war period. On 1 July 1946, Singapore became a separate Crown Colony from the Straits Settlements, with its own Governor and Director of Education.[2] At the suggestion of the Colonial Office in London, the British government introduced the 10-Year Plan in 1947 which advocated giving equal educational opportunity to all children.

---

[1] J. B. Neilson, *Annual Report of the Department of Education 1946,* Singapore: Government Printing Office, 1947, p. 7.
[2] Theodore R. Doraisamy (ed.), *150 Years of Education in Singapore,* Singapore: Stamford College Press Ltd, 1969, p. 45.

The 10-Year Plan can be seen as the response of the British government to a few challenges in the post-war educational scene. Firstly, there was 'the growing [British] consciousness of the need to relate education to the development of a new, if not yet clearly defined, nation-state' though 'the nation perceived was pan-Malayan rather than Singaporean'.[3] This was in part due to Britain's intent of granting self-government and eventual independence to her colonies in accordance with the Atlantic Charter of 1941. Secondly, Singapore saw an enormous demand for education as parents now seemed to desire an education for their children, a situation compounded by the post-war population increase. The response of the British administration indicated that it was now widely held that education should be available to all as a matter of right, instead of the privilege of a small group of people.[4] Furthermore, the system of separate schools for each of the four major language groups meant a lack of a common identity essential for the constitutional progress of Singapore. This was exacerbated by the rapid rise of private English stream, Chinese stream and Tamil stream schools. The Chinese stream schools were of particular concern as they were unwilling to accept the conditions attached to grants-in-aid, and the schools consciously fostered loyalties towards China.[5]

The 10-Year Plan thus articulated a long-term education policy based on equity and opportunity for all:

(a) That education should aim at fostering and extending the capacity for self-government, and the ideal of civic loyalty and responsibility.

(b) That equal educational opportunity should be afforded to the children — both boys and girls — of all races.

---

[3] H. E. Wilson, *Social Engineering in Singapore: Educational Policies and Social Change 1819–1972*, Singapore: Singapore University Press, 1978, p. 117.

[4] Ibid., p. 125. Wilson provided the background for the British administration's change in educational policy. In the UK, the *White Paper on Educational Reconstruction of 1943* indicated that it was Great Britain's responsibility 'to secure for children a happier childhood and a better start in life; to ensure a fuller measure of education and opportunity for young people and to provide means for all developing the various talents at which they are endowed…'. The 1944 Education Act provided for compulsory education between the ages of five and fifteen. In Singapore, principle of 'education for all' was accepted by the British Administration.

[5] Ibid., p. 127.

(c) That upon a basis of free primary education, there should be developed such as secondary, vocational and higher education as will best meet the needs of the country.[6]

With this, the British government propounded the policy of free elementary education for six years. Increased expenditure was given to the building of primary schools, teacher training and development of syllabuses and textbooks.

The British 10-Year Plan of 1946 provided for an extensive development of ' "post-primary" schools which were to be fee-paying, and admission to which would be restricted to pupils from primary schools which had reached "the prescribed standard of attainment" '.[7] However, with the emphasis placed on universally available elementary education, the extension of secondary education facilities failed to keep pace with demand, particularly for the vernacular streams.[8] Indeed, in 1955, only slightly more than half of the pupils from government primary schools were promoted to academic and technical secondary schools and a much higher proportion from aided English schools.[9] Even then, the teaching resources for secondary schools were straining the teaching resources of Singapore to the limit.[10]

In particular, there was a 'complete absence of post-primary education facilities for students from government Malay schools and aided or private Tamil schools'.[11] The Chinese stream schools followed China's 6-3-3 system of six years of primary education followed by three years in junior middle school and three years in senior middle school. Prior to 1949, graduates of Chinese stream schools pursued higher education in China. Following the establishment of communist rule in 1949, Chinese parents in Singapore were hesitant to send their children to China for higher education. The prospects were much better for English

---

[6] *Education Policy in Singapore. Ten Years' Programme 1947*, Singapore: Department of Education, 1947.

[7] H. E. Wilson, *Social Engineering in Singapore: Educational Policies and Social Change 1819–1972*, Singapore: Singapore University Press, 1978, p. 130.

[8] Ibid., pp. 135–136.

[9] *White Paper on Education Policy*, Legislative Assembly of Singapore, Sessional Paper, No. Cmd. 15 of 1956, p. 10.

[10] Ibid., p. 11.

[11] H. E. Wilson, *Social Engineering in Singapore: Educational Policies and Social Change 1819–1972*, Singapore: Singapore University Press, 1978, p. 145.

stream schools whose secondary school students had the option of sitting the Cambridge School Certificate and Higher School Certificate examinations and subsequent access to higher education.

While the British 10-Year Plan for education advocated equal educational opportunities for children of all races, in reality this was not so. Though grants-in-aid to vernacular schools continued, more resources, however, went towards promoting English stream education, which was to engender a fear of 'cultural extinction', particularly among the Chinese community. The continuation of different examinations, such as the School Certificate examination for English stream students, and the examinations offered by Chinese stream schools, with their different certificates offering differing employment prospects, only reinforced social division among the local people.

In 1955, Singapore attained limited internal self-government. With this, the Singapore government converted the British Department of Education to Singapore's Ministry of Education (MOE).[12] In the same year, against the background of Chinese pupils' involvement in political agitation and unrest, the All-Party Committee on Chinese Education in Singapore was appointed to investigate and make recommendations for Chinese education in Singapore.[13] In 1956, a *White Paper on Education Policy* was submitted to the Legislative Council. For the first time, Singaporean leaders led in formulating a national educational policy, laying the foundations for a national education system. It was significant that Mr Lee Kuan Yew was a member of the All-Party Committee, as the electoral success of the People's Action Party (PAP) in the 1959 elections meant the continued acceptance of the principles recommended by the All-Party Committee.[14]

The All-Party Committee presented two great educational problems confronting the government, as follows:

(a) To reconcile those elements of diversity which arose from the multi-racial structure of its population; and

---

[12] Theodore R. Doraisamy (ed.), *150 Years of Education in Singapore*, Singapore: Stamford College Press Ltd, 1969, p. 56.
[13] Ibid., p. 50.
[14] S. Gopinathan, *Towards A National System of Education in Singapore 1945–1973*. Singapore: Oxford University Press, 1974, p. 19.

(b) To cope with the phenomenal increase in the population of school-going age.[15]

Forging a common Malayan identity in the plural society is unlike that in most other countries where nearly all pupils are of one race and speak one language.[16] One of the most far-reaching recommendations of the Committee, inter alia, was for education policy to have equal respect for the four principal cultures in Singapore. Therefore, every parent should have the right to send his child to an English stream school, a Chinese stream school, a Malay stream school or a Tamil stream school.[17] All schools should also use similar Malayan-centred syllabuses, with textbooks specially written in the various local languages for this purpose.[18]

EXAMINATIONS DURING THE POST-WAR PERIOD

Primary School Examinations

Prior to and after World War II, there was some form of competitive examination for selection of pupils from government English stream primary schools for places in the few government English stream secondary schools. English primary schools provided for six years of primary education.[19] The expansion of free English primary school education saw the need for an equitable system of selection to secondary schools. In 1952, the Secondary School Entrance Examination (then known as the Common Standard VI Entrance Examination) was inaugurated. In 1958, the aided schools also joined the examination.[20] Up to 1959, however, the Secondary School Entrance Examination catered for the English stream only.

In the Malay stream primary schools, after the war, promotion from each class was based on examinations. The examinations for Standard

---

[15] *White Paper on Education Policy,* Legislative Assembly of Singapore, Sessional Paper, No. Cmd.15 of 1956, p. 4.

[16] Ibid.

[17] Ibid., p. 5.

[18] Ibid., p. 4.

[19] *First Education Triennial Survey Covering the Years 1955–7 Inclusive.* Singapore: Government Printing Office, 1959, p. 17.

[20] *A Short Account of PSLE, 1960–1970,* Singapore: Examinations Division, Ministry of Education, Nov 1970.

IV, V and VI were set by the Inspector of Schools and Assistant Inspector of Malay Schools, after consultation with Head Teachers.[21] In 1959, a common examination for pupils in Darjah VII was introduced, intended for admission to the first Malay secondary school classes.[22]

In the Chinese stream primary schools, the curriculum was a modified version of that used in China. In 1935, an annual common examination was implemented at the final year (6th year) of primary school and 3rd year of Junior Middle III. In 1951, the Primary 6 examination was dropped, but Junior Middle III examination was retained. In the same year, a new Senior Middle III examination at the end of the six-year post-primary education was implemented.[23]

In the Tamil stream primary schools, the Federation of Malaya Standard VII (Tamil) examination was a common examination for the pupils reaching Standard VII. There was no separate examination for the small numbers of pupils in Singapore.[24]

Secondary School Examinations

Following the return of British rule after the Japanese surrender, the Cambridge School Certificate examinations were immediately restored. An overwhelming number of candidates sat for the first post-war Cambridge examinations, which was a resounding success, as noted by the University of Cambridge Local Examinations Syndicate (UCLES):

> The Local Examinations Syndicate at its meeting today noted with pleasure the high standard achieved by the candidates from the Malayan Union and Singapore in the December, 1946 School Certificate Examination in spite of the adverse conditions under which they had been working. The Syndicate wishes to

[21] J. B. Neilson, *Annual Report of the Department of Education 1947*, Singapore: Government Printing Office, 1948, p. 28.

[22] *Ministry of Education Annual Report 1959*, Singapore: Government Printing Office, 1961, p. 4.

[23] *Department of Education Annual Report 1951*, Singapore: Government Printing Office, 1952, p. 17.

[24] The Federation of Malaya examination is also known as the Preparatory Examination for Tamil Teachers in *First Education Triennial Survey Covering the Years 1955–7 Inclusive*. Singapore: Government Printing Office, 1959, p. 33.

congratulate you and all concerned on the results in this, the first examination since the end of the war.[25]

From 1946 onwards, the English secondary schools resumed the Cambridge School Certificate, the predecessor of today's Singapore-Cambridge General Certificate of Education (GCE) Ordinary Level (O-Level).

The English secondary schools provided for four years of education, ending at the level of the Cambridge School Certificate. The general school curriculum included subjects such as English, History, Geography, Mathematics, General Science and Health Science. In the higher classes, students could take pure science subjects such as Physics, Chemistry and Biology. Optional subjects include Art, Religious Knowledge and Oriental Languages.[26] The better students who passed the Cambridge School Certificate progressed to a two-year Form VI course ending at the level of the Higher School Certificate,[27] the predecessor of today's Singapore-Cambridge GCE Advanced Level (A Level).

The choice of the Cambridge School Certificate and Higher School Certificate as examinations in English stream schools brought several advantages. Books were readily available to students, as the syllabuses were largely the same as those used in the United Kingdom (UK). Students were able to prepare for the School Certificate and Higher School Certificate examinations as past years' examination papers were available. The Higher School Certificate was accepted by the University of Malaya as its entrance examination.[28] The Higher School Certificate, being the qualification for admission to UK universities, opened up access to British higher education for those who could afford it or were awarded scholarships. Up to the 1970s, the results for candidates who took the Cambridge School Certificate and Higher School Certificate examinations were published in the newspapers. As the candidature increased, *The Straits Times* published pages and pages of examination results over several days, giving the names of candidates and their

[25] J. B. Neilson, *Annual Report of the Department of Education 1946,* Singapore: Government Printing Office, 1947, p. 20.

[26] *First Education Triennial Survey Covering the Years 1955–7 Inclusive.* Singapore: Government Printing Office, 1959, p. 37.

[27] Ibid., p. 17.

[28] Ibid.

overall examination results for all in Singapore and Malaya to see! The extensive use of the School Certificate and Higher School Certificate also helped to build a core of English-speaking Singaporeans and helped established the English language as the main working language in administration and business. This was to become one of Singapore's competitive strengths in modern times.

The use of the School Certificate and Higher School Certificate as the only examinations was not without its drawbacks. As the syllabuses were drawn up by UCLES, the curriculum was Anglo-centric. Students offering subjects such as Mathematics and Science, for example, had to deal with a plethora of units of measurement — from imperial measures such as pounds, miles and pints to metric units such as grammes, kilometres and litres. The fact the imperial measures were non-decimal and the absence of electronic calculators added to the learning load. However, students were able to quickly 'convert' 30 miles per hour to 44 feet per second, 45 miles per hour to 66 feet per second and 60 miles per hour to 88 feet per second. It helped that cars and trains often travelled at 30 miles per hour, 45 miles per hour or 60 miles per hour, at least in the Mathematics and Science examination papers!

A Plethora of Units...

The Imperial system is based on the foot, pound, second (FPS) as units for length, mass and time whereas the metric system was based on the centimetre, gramme, second (CGS). The CGS system was later replaced by the MKS system, i.e., metre, kilogram, second.

In the Science syllabuses, different units of force and energy were also used — one for FPS, one for CGS and one for MKS.

In the FPS system, there were 2 types of units of force — the poundal and the pound-weight. The poundal was the force needed to cause a mass of 1 pound to accelerate at 1 foot/second^2, whereas the pound-weight was the force of gravity acting on a mass of 1 pound. In the CGS system, the unit of force was the dyne, being the force needed to cause a mass of 1 gramme to accelerate at 1 centimetre/second^2.

Test yourself ...

1 What is the foot-poundal?
2 Convert the pound-weight to poundal.
3 What is your weight in stones?

**Excerpts from the Oversea School Certificate (December 1958) ©
UCLES**[29]

For Mathematics Paper I, students needed to learn how to calculate
using pounds, shillings and pence.

6. A tea merchant mixes two kinds of tea costing 5*s*. and 7*s*. 6*d*. per lb. in
the ratio 3:2 by weight. Find his profit per cent. if he sells the mixture at 8*s*.
per lb.

The price of the 5*s*. tea goes up by 10 per cent., and that of the 7*s*. 6*d*. tea
goes up by 20 per cent. If, by selling a mixture at 8*s*. 8*d*. per lb., the merchant
intends to make the same percentage profit as before, find in what ratio he
must now mix the two kinds of tea.

For Additional Mathematics Paper II, students needed to work with
British units of measurement.

7. In 10 sec. a certain machine lifts a load of 400 lb. through a vertical distance
of 10 ft. and gives it a velocity of 8 ft. per sec. Calculate in ft. lb.-wt. the work
done on the load. If the machine is 40% efficient, find the average horse-
power at which it is working.

Besides the Anglo-centric nature of the School Certificate and Higher
School Certificate, the use of the School Certificate was to have
unintended consequences for Singapore education in later years. This
was because the School Certificate and its replacement, the GCE O-Level,
was intended for the top 20%[30] of the UK cohort and were offered mainly
by students in grammar schools after five years of secondary schooling.
Unfortunately, this examination became the sole examination available
for all English stream students in Singapore.

For the Chinese stream secondary schools, the Government Senior
Middle III Examination, organised by MOE, was the common school-
leaving examination. The curriculum included Chinese Language,
Chinese Literature, English, Geography, History, Mathematics and
Science. This examination was taken after three years in Junior Middle

[29] *Oversea School Certificate Examination Papers 1958*, UK: Cambridge University Press, 1959. ©
UCLES
[30] Sir J. Waddell, *Report of the Steering Committee Established to Consider Proposals for Replacing the
General Certificate of Education Ordinary-Level and Certificate of Secondary Education Examinations
by a Common System of Examining*, July 1978, p. 2.

School and three years in Senior Middle School. It was the basic qualification for entry to Chinese teacher training classes and to certain government posts. Those who attained good results could be admitted to Form VI classes in English schools, in preparation for the Cambridge Higher School Certificate.[31]

The absence of Malay stream and Tamil stream secondary schools prior to 1960 meant that there were no common examinations in these two language streams as well.[32] The majority of the pupils left school before the end of the seven years of primary school.[33]

CONCLUSION

On the eve of self-government in 1959, education and examinations in Singapore remained fragmented along language lines. The English stream schools enjoyed a well-articulated path from primary schools to secondary schools, with terminal examinations in the form of the Cambridge School Certificate and Higher School Certificate. Chinese stream education had terminal examinations in the form of the Senior Middle III Examination. Other than primary education, there were no Malay or Tamil secondary schools. Such were the challenges confronting the PAP government upon attaining self-government.

---

[31] *First Education Triennial Survey Covering the Years 1955–7 Inclusive.* Singapore: Government Printing Office, 1959, pp. 38 & 41.

[32] After the PAP government took over in 1959, Malay stream secondary classes were started at Kallang, Monk's Hill, Siglap, Serangoon and Geylang Craft Centre. In 1960, the Umar Pulavar Tamil School was upgraded to become the first aided Tamil secondary school. In Theodore R. Doraisamy (ed.), *150 Years of Education in Singapore*, Singapore: Stamford College Press Ltd, 1969, pp. 112 & 121.

[33] *Department of Education Annual Report 1952*, Singapore: Government Printing Office, 1953, p. 30.

CHAPTER

Why and how effective were the measures undertaken by the Singapore government to establish central control over education and examinations in Singapore in the 1960s and 1970s?

If in the four different languages of instruction, we teach our children four different standards of right and wrong, four different ideal patterns of behaviour, then we will produce four different groups of people and there will be no integrated coherent society.[1]

Mr Lee Kuan Yew
The then Prime Minister of Singapore, 1959

This was the challenge faced by the People's Action Party (PAP) government after Singapore attained full internal self-government. Thus, in the 1960s and 1970s, the government moved towards a national educational system. In 1959, after Singapore gained internal self-government, the aims of the education policy were as follows:

(a) Equal treatment for the four streams, namely Malay, Chinese, Tamil and English;

(b) Establishment of four official languages with Malay as the national language of the new nation in an attempt to unify the multi-racial community;

(c) Emphasis on the study of Mathematics, Science, and technical subjects designed to equip the youth with requisite skills, aptitudes and attitudes for employment in the industrial sector; and

(d) Building of loyalty to the nation.[2]

---

[1] The then Prime Minister Lee Kuan Yew's speech, *The Straits Times*, 9 December 1959, quoted in Jason Tan, S. Gopinathan & W. K. Ho, *Education in Singapore: A Book of Readings*, Singapore: Simon & Schuster (Asia), 1997, p. 41.

[2] Goh Keng Swee, *Report on the Ministry of Education, 1978*, Singapore: Ministry of Education, 10 February 1979, p. 2–1.

By recognising the diversity of the races and parity of the four languages, the Singapore government 'could take credit for removing some of the causes of tension which [had] set people apart'[3] during the colonial period. At the same time, to bring the divergent tendencies together, the government prescribed common curricula and standards for the four language streams, centralised training by the Teachers' Training College and exercised central supervision of schools by Ministry of Education (MOE).[4] In addition, the government instituted the flag-raising ceremony and the singing of the national anthem in all schools so as to promote a common sense of identity in the pupils. The bilingual policy, which became the cornerstone of Singapore's education system, was adopted. In the words of the then Prime Minister, Mr Lee Kuan Yew:

> Singapore never had one common language. It was a polyglot community under colonial rule.... We realized that English had to be the language of the workplace and common language. As an international trading community, we would not make a living if we used Malay, Chinese or Tamil.... I introduced the teaching of three mother tongues in English schools...the teaching of English in Chinese, Malay and Tamil schools....[5]

To further provide opportunities for interaction among the different races, the government set up the Integrated Schools, which represented the first step towards the building of a national school system. The first of these schools was the Bukit Panjang Government High School (BPGHS), formed by the merger of Bukit Panjang Secondary School and the Chua Chu Kang Government Chinese Middle School and functioning in the same school building.

From the start, BPGHS was an experiment that defied failure. When the school opened its doors on 11 January 1960, it made history as the first integrated government secondary school in Singapore. Two different language streams, Chinese and English were run by a single administration under one roof with students sharing classrooms and

---

[3] H. E. Wilson, *Social Engineering in Singapore, 1942–1945: Educational Policies and Social Change 1819–1972*, Singapore: Singapore University Press, 1978, p. 229.
[4] *Ministry of Education Annual Report 1959*, Singapore: Government Printing Office, 1961, p. 1.
[5] Lee Kuan Yew, *From Third World to First: The Singapore Story: 1965–2000*, Singapore: Singapore Press Holdings, 2000, pp. 169–170.

Bukit Panjang Government High School – View of school building and ground (Courtesy of the National Archives of Singapore).

teachers doing the same in the common room. The challenge for the school was to foster integration between the English and Chinese educated students — something it did with panache and imagination through extra curricular activities such as folk dancing.[6]

THE PRIMARY SCHOOL LEAVING EXAMINATION

The introduction of common curricula and common standards for all four language streams paved the way for the setting up of a national system of examinations for the first time in the history of the island. In 1960, the Primary School Leaving Examination (PSLE) was inaugurated in four official languages — English, Chinese, Malay and Tamil — for Primary 6 pupils, at about 12 years of age, with the main purpose of selecting and placing pupils in secondary schools. This common examination was managed by a consultative committee for each language stream and a coordinating committee comprising MOE officials, principals and teachers of the four language streams. These two committees advised on the dates of the examination as well as the scope and weighting for each subject. Common examination subjects were prescribed by the Ministry: First Language, Second Language, Mathematics, Science, History and Geography. The question papers were centrally set by MOE and scoring done by appointed school teachers using common

[6] http://www.bpghs.moe.edu.sg/history.htm

standards. Common certification and thus equal opportunity for access to post-primary education were accorded for the four language streams, unlike the British period where the English certification carried more prestige and opportunities for its pupils.

A total of 30,615 candidates sat for this first examination. Overall, 45% of the candidates passed the examination. The percentage passes by language streams were as follows:[7]

Language Streams	Percentage Passes
English Medium	34%
Chinese Medium	68%
Malay Medium	47%
Tamil Medium	57%

The low percentage of passes obtained in the English medium was due to the automatic promotion system which prevailed in the past but ceased from 1960.[8] Pupils, who did not pass the PSLE either had to repeat (26%), be posted to Secondary 1 classes (10%) or Post-Primary classes (18%) or be superannuated (1%).[9]

The high percentage of failure rates in the PSLE caused some concern. A 1963 Commission of Inquiry into Education in Singapore found that the failure rates ranged from 32% to 52% in 1962.[10] Furthermore, as a selection examination, the PSLE was set at a standard at which only 47% of the English stream candidates and 68% in the Chinese stream could pass.[11] The Commission thus called for the revision of the PSLE to serve as a qualifying examination to assess the progress and attainment of the pupils, and as a selection examination to channel pupils to the different secondary courses.[12] Consequently, the PSLE was set at a standard at which 80%, or 4 out of 5 candidates would be able to pass.[13]

---

[7] *Ministry of Education Annual Report 1960*, Singapore: Government Printing Office, 1962, p. 6.
[8] Ibid.
[9] Ibid.
[10] *Commission of Inquiry into Education, Singapore. Final Report*, 28 August 1963, Singapore: Government Printing Office, 1964, p. 24.
[11] Ibid., p. 26.
[12] Ibid.
[13] Ibid., p. 27.

EXAMINATIONS IN SECONDARY SCHOOLS IN THE 1960s

The 1960s saw a certain degree of uniformity for examinations in secondary schools (through the School Certificate Examination) and post-secondary schools (through the Higher School Certificate Examination), as these common certifications were recognised for educational advancement and employment, albeit in different language streams. The requirement for bilingualism also imposed some commonality across the secondary school examinations. From 1966, Secondary 1 students were required to learn a second language. In 1966, Second Language was offered as an examination at School Certificate.

English Stream Schools

The English stream schools continued with the use of the Cambridge School Certificate and Higher School Certificate.[14] The Cambridge School Certificate was awarded to candidates who had passed in the English Language in Group 1 and satisfactory standards obtained in at least three other groups of subjects.[15] In 1959, the General Certificate of Education (GCE) was instituted for the first time in Singapore. The GCE was awarded to candidates who, although not qualifying for the award of the Cambridge School Certificate, had attained credit in at least three subjects. The holders of GCE were permitted to take the Higher School Certificate.[16] The GCE was also recognised by the Singapore government as alternative qualification for entry to government service and Teachers' Training College.[17] In 1965, the GCE was awarded for the first time to all candidates who had passed with credit in at least one subject.[18]

---

[14] The Higher School Certificate (English) was first examined in 1951. In *Department of Education Annual Report 1951*, Singapore: Government Printing Office, 1952, p. 85.

[15] Press release *Analysis of 1961 Cambridge School Certificate Examination*, Singapore: Ministry of Education (through Ministry of Culture), 19 March 1962.

[16] Ibid.

[17] Press release *Results of the Joint Examination for the Cambridge School Certificate, the Federation of Malaya Certificate and the General Certificate of Education, 1962*, Singapore: Ministry of Education, 11 March 1963.

[18] Press release *Results of the Joint Examination for the Cambridge School Certificate, Malaysia Certificate of Education and the General Certificate of Education, 1965*, Singapore: Ministry of Education, 26 February 1966.

Deputy Prime Minister Dr Toh Chin Chye speaks at the meeting of the Singapore Advisory of the University of Cambridge Local Examinations Syndicate at the Ministry of Education. (Ministry of Information, Communications and The Arts, courtesy of the National Archives of Singapore.)

The value of the Cambridge School Certificate was articulated by Dr Toh Chin Chye, the then Deputy Prime Minister:

> The Cambridge School Certificate Examination is unique, having had 80 years of history in Singapore. During this time, proconsuls have come and gone and politics have taken a new colouring, but like a certain brand of Scotch whisky, the Cambridge School Certificate Examination is still going strong.[19]

But Dr Toh also expressed a desire for an examination that is more suited for Singapore:

> I do not see therefore a replacement of the Cambridge School Certificate and the HSC examination in the near future, but it would be helpful to us if these examinations...can be adapted to our changing circumstances and needs as an independent country.[20]

---

[19] Speech by the Deputy Prime Minister, Dr Toh Chin Chye, at the meeting of the Singapore Advisory Commitee of the University of Cambridge Local Examinations Syndicate, 16 May 1964.
[20] Ibid.

Chinese Stream Schools

There was, however, still a divide between the structure of the English stream schools and the Chinese stream schools, as the latter continued with a 6-3-3 system, i.e., six years of primary, three years of junior middle and three years of senior middle school — the same structure as China's education system while English stream schools operated on a 6-4-2 system, i.e., six years of primary, four years of secondary and two years of pre-university education. Both systems had different examinations. In the context of creating uniformity for all four language streams, the government moved to standardise secondary education for the Chinese stream schools with that of the English stream. In Dec 1961, MOE conducted the first Government Secondary IV School Certificate Examination side-by-side with the Senior Middle III Examination for the Chinese stream schools.[21] This effort to harmonise the two structures was exploited by communists and pro-communists elements for their own ends. (See Chapter 6 for the 1961 Chinese examination boycott.)

The standardisation of English and Chinese education systems saw the end of unequal treatment between English and Chinese school-leavers. The latter could enjoy the same recognition and status for government employment and teaching training after completing the Government Secondary IV School Certificate (Chinese) after four years, instead of the Senior Middle III after six years.[22]

In 1963, the first Higher School Certificate (Chinese) Examination was conducted. MOE, in conjunction with the University of Singapore and the Nanyang University, set up the examination syllabuses for this examination.[23]

Malay Stream Schools

Malay stream secondary schools did not exist in the pre-war period. Doraisamy saw 'the establishment of Malay secondary schools as the

---

[21] Theodore R. Doraisamy (ed.), *150 Years of Education in Singapore*, Singapore: Stamford College Press Ltd, 1969, p. 77.
[22] Ibid., p. 61.
[23] Ibid., p. 76.

first step in the educational provision for the Malays to achieve social mobility and economic advancement'. The Sang Nila Utama Secondary School was the first Malay secondary school to be completed and opened.[24] Soon after the PAP government came into power in 1959, Malay stream secondary classes were started.[25] The secondary students sat for the Federation of Malaya Certificate of Education (Malay) in 1963, subsequently replaced by the Malaysia Certificate of Education in 1964 and School Certificate (Malay) in 1969.[26] From 1966, the Higher School Certificate (Malay) was also offered to post-secondary students.[27]

Tamil Stream Schools

In 1960, the first aided Tamil secondary school was established.[28] From 1963, the School Certificate (Tamil) Examination was conducted for the first time for school candidates only. From 1964 onwards, private candidates were allowed to take the examination. The School Certificate (Tamil) Examination was given the same recognition as that of the Government Secondary IV School Certificate (Chinese) and the Cambridge School Certificate (English). Students who passed English as second language were eligible to enter pre-university classes in English stream secondary schools.[29]

Other Examinations

In addition to the mainstream School Certificate and Higher School Certificate examinations, MOE also coordinated a number of other examinations, as shown in its 1963 Annual Report:[30]

---

[24] *Ministry of Education Annual Report 1961*, Singapore: Government Printing Office, 1962, p. 2.
[25] Theodore R. Doraisamy (ed.), *150 Years of Education in Singapore*, Singapore: Stamford College Press Ltd, 1969, p. 112.
[26] *Ministry of Education Annual Report 1963*, Singapore: Government Printing Office, 1965, p. 8.
[27] Theodore R. Doraisamy (ed.), *150 Years of Education in Singapore*, Singapore: Stamford College Press Ltd, 1969, p. 112.
[28] Ibid., p. 123.
[29] Ibid., p. 122.
[30] *Ministry of Education Annual Report 1963*, Singapore: Government Printing Office, pp. 8–15.

- National Language Public Examinations;[31]

- Special Language Examinations in Chinese, Tamil and English;[32]

- General Certificate of Education of the Associated Examining Board;[33]

- London Chamber of Commerce Examination;[34]

- City and Guilds of the London Institute (Technical Examinations);

- Associated Board of the Royal Schools of Music;

- Examinations of the University of Queensland, the Royal Melbourne Technical College and the Department of Education of New South Wales held under the Colombo Plan Correspondence Scheme;

- Degree examinations of the University of London;

- Bar examinations of the Council of Legal Education; and

- Examinations of the Association of Certified and Corporate Accountants, the Institute of Cost and Works Accountants, the National Institute of Accountants, the Corporation of Secretaries, the Institute of Chartered Shipbrokers, the Institute of Work Study, the Rating and Valuation Association, the Institute of Taxation, the Co-operative Union Ltd., the British Institute of Management.

TOWARDS STANDARDISATION OF SECONDARY EXAMINATIONS IN THE 1970s

The Singapore-Cambridge GCE Ordinary Level (O-Level) Examination

A decade after the introduction of a common PSLE for all language

---

[31] First examined in 1959. In *Ministry of Education Annual Report 1961*, Singapore: Government Printing Office, 1962, p. 6.

[32] First examined in 1962. In *Ministry of Education Annual Report 1962*, Singapore: Government Printing Office, 1964, p. 9.

[33] Ceased to be examined in 1963. In *Ministry of Education Annual Report 1963*, Singapore: Government Printing Office, p. 13.

[34] Outram Secondary School presented candidates for the London Chamber of Commerce Examination for the last time in 1963. Thereafter, the school presented candidates for commercial subjects in the Cambridge School Certificate Examination. In *Ministry of Education Annual Report 1963*, Singapore: Government Printing Office, p. 14.

streams in primary schools, it was timely that a common examination be introduced for the secondary schools as well. This was the Singapore-Cambridge GCE O-Level Examination, first introduced in 1971. This certificate, jointly issued by MOE and the University of Cambridge Local Examinations Syndicate (UCLES), replaced the Cambridge School Certificate, Government Secondary IV School Certificate (Chinese), School Certificate (Malay) and School Certificate (Tamil). UCLES was responsible for the examinations and standards examined in English; and MOE, for examinations and standards examined in Chinese, Malay and Tamil, and the subject English as a second language.[35] The certificate was awarded to candidates who had passed in at least one subject at Ordinary Pass with Grades from 1 to 6 (formerly known as credit passes). Grades 7 and 8 represented standards below an O-Level pass. According to Mr Cheong Hock Hai, the then Chief Examinations Officer, the new examination was the inevitable result of the historical evolution of secondary school examinations, as the four parallel certificates were untidy. The new certificate was a new national award reflecting the parity of the four streams and similar academic standards.[36]

The Singapore-Cambridge GCE Advanced Level (A-Level) Examination

In 1975, the Singapore-Cambridge GCE A-Level Certificate replaced the Higher School Certificates, conducted for all language streams. The A-Level examination was conducted by MOE in collaboration with UCLES. MOE was responsible for the subjects examined in the Mother Tongue languages. For the rest of the subjects, UCLES was the examining authority and oversaw the development of syllabuses, setting of examination papers, marking of answer scripts and awarding of grades.

What's the Difference: School Certificate and O-Levels

Prior to 1971, students in the English stream schools offered the Cambridge School Certificate Examination. In 1971, Singapore switched to the Singapore-

---

[35] *Examinations Division Annual Report 1971*, Singapore: Ministry of Education, 1971.
[36] Cheong Hock Hai, *The Singapore-Cambridge General Certificate of Education*, Singapore: Ministry of Education.

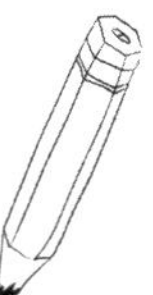

Cambridge General Certificate of Education (GCE) Ordinary Level (O-Level) Examination, an examination that continues to today.

The School Certificate was a grouped certificate in that subjects were placed in different groups and candidates were required to offer subjects from the various groups. English Language was a compulsory subject and in a group on its own. Other subjects were grouped as General Subjects (e.g., History, Geography), Mathematical Subjects (Mathematics, Additional Mathematics), Science Subjects (e.g., Physics, Chemistry), Arts and Crafts (e.g., Art, Music, Woodwork) and Technical & Commercial Subjects (e.g., Geometrical & Mechanical Drawing, Principles of Accounts). Candidates were required to offer at least six subjects, which must include English Language and subjects selected from at least three of the groups. To qualify for a School Certificate, candidates must pass in at least six subjects (including English Language) with at least a credit, or pass in five subjects (including English Language) with credit in at least two subjects. Candidates were also awarded a First Division, a Second Division or a Third Division School Certificate, depending on their performance. For example, to qualify for a First Division School Certificate, a candidate must obtain a credit in English Language, and subjects in at least three other groups.

The School Certificate, with its subject group system, was seen as too rigid, as the success of the candidate was based on the group and not the individual subject as a unit. It required candidates to select subjects from specific groups of subjects at a time when the range of subjects increased. In the United Kingdom (UK), the School Certificate was replaced in 1951 by the General Certificate of Education Ordinary Level Examination (O-Levels).

The UK O-Levels was a single subject examination. There were no compulsory subjects or restrictions on subject combinations. This allowed students to drop their weak subject and hence demonstrate better achievement. A student who passed in at least one subject would be awarded a certificate. Thus, performance at the O-Levels was measured by the number of subjects passed (e.g., passed with three or more O-Levels, passed with five or more O-Levels).

The Singapore-Cambridge O-Levels was slightly different in that certain subjects were compulsory, e.g., English Language, Mother Tongue Languages. There were also certain requirements to ensure that students have a broad-based education (e.g., Combined Humanities was a compulsory subject). Students' choice of subjects was also influenced to a large extent by the admission criteria to junior colleges (First Language and five Relevant Subjects) and polytechnics. Thus, while there was some flexibility in the choice of subjects, the Singapore-Cambridge O-Levels retained some elements of the School Certificate in that candidates need to offer subjects from broad categories of subjects (e.g., Humanities, Science & Mathematics).

There were no requirements that candidates need to pass in subjects from specific groups to earn a certificate.

What are National Examinations?

National examinations refer to centrally coordinated and common examinations for all school-leaving pupils at the end of a specific stage of education within the context of a national education system. In Singapore, national examinations were introduced in 1960, with the implementation of the PSLE at primary level, for the four official language streams. This was an outcome of the introduction of the national school system that brought together schools of the four language streams, under a unified education system, with a common curriculum, common provision of physical and financial resources. The PSLE unified the different school-leaving examinations of government and aided schools that existed prior to 1960, with a common examination for schools under the different language streams. Similarly, the Singapore Cambridge General Certificate of Education Ordinary Level introduced at secondary level in 1971 and Singapore-Cambridge General Certificate of Education Advanced Level at pre-university level in 1975 were aimed at bringing secondary and pre-university examinations under common certifications. These national examinations served as common examinations for all school-leaving pupils, albeit under different language streams, for purposes of selection for higher education and recognition for employment. In the national examinations of the 1960s and 1970s, pupils have the choice of offering subjects in one of the four languages, and either English or Mother Tongue as first or second language. The national stream was introduced in 1983, as a result of the overwhelming preference of parents for an English-medium education.[37]

CONCLUSION

Since 1960, national examinations have played an important role in the Singapore education system. The question of whether the curriculum drives examinations or examinations drive the curriculum had surfaced in the British period as to whether the Cambridge examinations led to cramming. It also re-surfaced in the 1963 Commission of Inquiry into Education. Under the section on 'dangers of external examinations':

> There is a body of influential opinion which considers that the teaching of school pupils with a view to achieving examination

---

[37] Diana Giam, *Indexes to Major Changes in Education in Singapore from 1979 to 1992*, Singapore: Ministry of Education, Library and Information Centre, June 1992, p. 7.

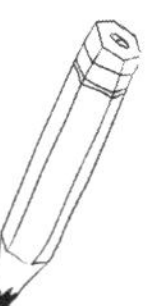

goals may conflict seriously with the teaching of those aspects of the subjects which are of educational value. In the Singapore schools, the defects of school education and classroom instruction arise from the nature of the syllabuses and the level and method of instruction. All these have tended to be dominated by examination requirements. This is particularly evident from Primary IV to Primary VI, where the aim of school teaching appears to be geared mainly to the requirements of the Primary School Leaving Examination.[38]

Yet, the Commission also acknowledged that external examinations have a constructive role to play.

> The stimulus of achieving recognised standards can have far reaching effects. It often improves performance in the more theoretical study. This is particularly true of the university entrance examination. Pupils take this examination as a definite means for special ends. This examination being selective, satisfies the urge to excel, as well as to achieve. Secondly the external examination serves to set a uniform standard for schools. In this way, the varying standards of different schools tend to be reduced, resulting in increasing uniformity of standards and achievement. Finally, an examination properly controlled can be a powerful aid to the teacher in keeping up with the growth in the content and knowledge of the different subjects. This is particularly relevant from the point of view of teachers on whom individually falls the duty of keeping up with their subjects.[39]

The PSLE and the GCE examinations are the pillars of the national examination system. The examinations assess students' ability and achievement and examination results are used to determine a student's progression from one level of education to the next. From 1960 onwards, candidates who met the standards required in the national examinations received a common certificate for education in Singapore. The efficacy of a common certificate for national unity was clear, as it reflected the

---

[38] Ibid., p. 26.
[39] Ibid., pp. 25–26.

parity and unity of Singapore's education system, and brought about the integration of the four language streams.[40]

National examinations have played an important role in contributing to the development of human capital in post-independent Singapore. Criticisms notwithstanding, national examinations have supported an education system aimed at providing a common educational experience for students from different communities. It seems national examinations have come of age, and are here to stay.

---

[40] Francis H. K. Wong & Y. H. Gwee, *Perspectives: The Development of Education in Malaysia and Singapore*, Kuala Lumpur, Singapore, Hong Kong: Heinmann Educational Books (Asia) Ltd, 1972, p. 90.

CHAPTER

The 1961 examination boycott illustrates the challenges in forging a national system of examinations. Do you agree?

The year 1961 was an important milestone in the implementation of Government's policy of equal treatment for the four streams of education... Unfortunately, the Government Secondary IV (Chinese) Examination was marred by a boycott staged by some misguided students who were instigated by adults for political reasons. The great majority of the students, as well as their parents, rallied in support of the Government. They ignored the insults of student pickets and risked bodily injury to make their way into the Examination Centres. That the boycott was a failure is proved by the fact that over 70 per cent of the candidates managed to sit for the examination.[1]

Ministry of Education (MOE)
Annual Report 1961

BACKGROUND TO THE EXAMINATION BOYCOTT

The background of the 1961 examination boycott was to be found in the politicisation of Chinese students and exploitation by communists and pro-communists in the post-war period. In and after 1954, there was a preponderance of news headlines on student unrest in the Chinese middle schools and involvement in industrial disputes.[2] In

---

[1] *Ministry of Education Annual Report 1961*, Singapore: Government Printing Office, 1962, p. 1.
[2] Theodore R. Doraisamy (ed.), *150 years of Education in Singapore*, Singapore: Stamford College Press Ltd., 1969, p. 92.

1954, Chinese students campaigned against the application of the National Service Ordinance.[3] In 1955, the students joined workers in the Hock Lee Bus Riots. In September 1956, after the government had banned seven communist-front organisations, including the Singapore Chinese Middle School Students' Union, 5,000 students staged a protest at six Chinese schools and rioted in many parts of the city, with 15 people killed and more than 100 injured. For two days, Singapore was under a curfew.[4] The *1956 White Paper* cited evidence that communist agents were involved in making contact with the students, although not through the school authorities or teachers.[5] In 1961, a change in policy regarding Chinese examinations was again exploited by the pro-communists for political ends.

When Singapore attained self-government in 1959, a key element of the government's educational policy was to accord parity for all language streams. At that time, the English stream schools followed a 6-4-2 system, i.e., six years of primary school, four years of secondary school and two years of pre-university. On the other hand, the Chinese stream system modelled the school system in China and followed the 6-3-3 system, i.e., six years of primary school, three years of junior middle school and three years of senior middle school. The Chinese stream schools were mainly influenced by developments in China, followed a different curriculum from the English stream schools and conducted their own examinations.

In the context of creating uniformity, the government moved to standardise the structure for all the four language streams. In 1960, the Primary School Leaving Examination (PSLE) was instituted for all four language streams. Subsequently, the government moved to standardise the secondary school examinations in Chinese stream schools with that of the English stream. The Chinese stream's 6-3-3 system was to be replaced by the 6-4-2 system, with four years at the secondary level and two years at the pre-university level, with examinations at the

[3] *First Education Triennial Survey Covering the Years 1955–7 Inclusive*, Singapore: Government Printing Office, 1959, p. 18.
[4] C. M. Turnbull, *A History of Singapore 1819–1988*, 2nd Ed., Singapore: Oxford University Press, 1996, p. 258.
[5] *First Education Triennial Survey Covering the Years 1955–7 Inclusive*, Singapore: Government Printing Office, 1959, p. 19.

end of Secondary 4 and pre-university level. MOE also took over the conduct of examinations from the individual secondary schools.[6] In December 1961, MOE conducted the first Government Secondary IV School Certificate Examination side-by-side with the Government Senior Middle III Examination.[7]

School Certificate (Chinese) Examination, 1961

[6] *Singapore: An Illustrated History 1941–1984*, Singapore: Information Division, Ministry of Culture, 1984, pp. 222, 233–235.
[7] Theodore R. Doraisamy (ed.), *150 years of Education in Singapore*, Singapore: Stamford College Press Ltd., 1969, p. 77.

THE EXAMINATION BOYCOTT

The Secondary IV Examination was scheduled for a week, from 27 November to 2 December 1961. On the first day of the examination (27 November), student pickets barricaded the gates and roads to all 18 examination centres, and form 'human chains' to keep candidates and their parents away from the examination centres. Banners and posters were put up and pamplets distributed to urge students to boycott the examinations. Despite that, the examination proceeded, although it started an hour late.[8] More than 60% (1,900 out of 3,000) of the candidates sat for the examination.[9] On the second day (28 November), an emergency centre was set up at the MOE headquarters, Kay Siang Road, for students who could not get to their own examination centres. At this centre, student pickets numbered about 300 students, the largest since the start of the boycott.[10] 1,500 candidates sat for examinations at the various centres.[11] The government agreed to provide police protection, but only upon request by parents and students who have decided to defy the pickets and sit for the examination.[12] By the third day (29 November), MOE had announced the setting up of 'mobile examination centres' to cater to any group of 50 or more candidates at any point in Singapore. The examinations ended a day earlier to 'lessen the strain on parents and candidates'.[13] About 54% (1,698 out of 3,150) of the candidates sat for the examinations.[14] On the fourth day (30 November), 83% of the candidates sat for the Additional Mathematics paper and 58% (1,449 out of 2,521) of the candidates sat for the Geography optional paper.[15] On the fifth and final day (1 December), 62% (1,958 out of 3,169) of the candidates sat for the examination.[16]

[8] *The Straits Times*, 28 November 1961, p. 1.
[9] *Legislative Assembly Debates State of Singapore*, Official Report, Third Session of the First Legislative Assembly, Part I of Third Session, from 31 October 1961 to 21 December 1961, Volume 15, Singapore: Government Printer, 1964, p. 766.
[10] *The Straits Times*, 29 November 1961, p. 1.
[11] *Legislative Assembly Debates State of Singapore*, Official Report, Third Session of the First Legislative Assembly, Part I of Third Session, from 31 October 1961 to 21 December 1961, Volume 15, Singapore: Government Printer, 1964, p. 810.
[12] *The Straits Times*, 29 November 1961, p. 1.
[13] *The Straits Times*, 30 November 1961, p. 20.
[14] *The Straits Times*, 30 November 1961, p. 20.
[15] *Legislative Assembly Debates State of Singapore*, Official Report, Third Session of the First Legislative Assembly, Part I of Third Session, from 31 October 1961 to 21 December 1961, Volume 15, Singapore: Government Printer, 1964, p. 971.
[16] Ibid., p. 1053.

During the course of the boycott, there were clashes between pickets, parents and candidates. Many candidates, escorted by their parents, had to push past picket lines and climb over or under the fences to get into the examination centres. In addition, the pickets held a school principal captive for some time, stuffed the exhaust pipe of an invigilator and cut off the telephone line of an examination centre.[17]

A Case of Mistaken Identity...[18]

On 27 November 1961, the then Minister of Education Mr Yong Nyuk Lin informed the Legislative Assembly that a University of Malaya graduate, Mr Tommy Koh Thong Bee (now Prof Tommy Koh, Ambassador-at-Large), among others, had visited Chinese schools to lend 'general support' to the examination boycott.

Mr Tommy Koh denied any involvement. Mr David Marshall told the Legislative Assembly that Mr Koh had contacted him by telephone from a hotel in the Cameron Highlands, Malaya. Mr Marshall added that at the time of the incident, Mr Koh was 'travelling between Kuala Lumpur and Tapah — more than 300 miles away from the Whampoa School'.[19]

On 28 Nov 1961, Mr Yong Nyuk Lin issued a full apology and described the circumstances leading to the mistaken identification of Mr Koh. He told the Legislative Assembly that a car bearing the registration plate SU4444 was seen turning into St George's Road and proceeding to Whampoa Road School examination centre. The car belonged to Mr Koh's father and a young Chinese sitting in the front seat was thought to be Mr Koh. It turned out to be a case of mistaken identity.

[17] *The Straits Times*, 30 November 1961, p. 20.
[18] *The Straits Times*, 29 November 1961, p. 11.
[19] *The Straits Times*, 29 November 1961, p. 11.

Examinations must go on...

Mr Koh Hoe Kuan was one of the dramatis personae in the events of the Chinese examination boycott that unfolded at the Ministry of Education headquarters, Kay Siang Road.

The Ministry of Education was a hot spot for defiant student pickets during the period of the Chinese examination boycott. An emergency centre had been set up at the Ministry for candidates who were intimidated by pickets and prevented from entering their own examination centres by 'human chains' of pickets. From the entrance of the Ministry to the buildings, there was also a 'human chain' of pickets. Meanwhile, the walls of the buildings had been pasted with posters inciting protest against the Secondary IV examinations. The then Chief Examinations Officer, Rev T. R. Doraisamy issued instructions for the posters to be removed. Mr Koh went out of the building cautiously while his examinations colleagues were standing outside the corridors of the examinations building, facing the chain of pickets along the road. In full view of the onlookers and unaided, Mr Koh took off the posters, with trembling hands. One picket actually ran up close and tried to snap a photo of Mr Koh. On recollection today, Mr Koh said of himself: 'Fools rushed in where angels feared to tread'.

Mr Koh was further tasked with cutting the fence facing Margaret Drive, as a standby arrangement, in case candidates were obstructed from entering the emergency examination centre. Late at night, he bided his time, did a surreptitious 'leopard crawl' up to the fence, cut the fence with a pair of pliers and tied it with twine. If the fence falls through, it will be big enough for one person to go through. All this while, he escaped the notice of pickets who were prowling along Margaret Drive late into the night. Having done the deed, he stayed overnight in the examinations office and when he took an occasional peek through the door, he saw one picket, face covered by handkerchief, cycling along the road.

During the period of the examination boycott, the pickets would congregate at the entrances to the Ministry in the morning. On one occasion, Mr Koh walked up to the pickets and told them 'you are students, we are workers here, let my colleagues in …'.

Mr Koh Hoe Kuan is the longest-serving member of Singapore's examinations staff. In 1958, he joined the Examinations Branch as a 19-year-old clerk. He served at the Cambridge Unit responsible for the administration of the School Certificate and Higher School Certificate. In 1964, he was awarded the Public Service Administration Medal (Silver), the only clerk to have won such distinction in recognition of his dedication during the 1961 examination boycott. In 1996, he was awarded the Long Service Medal. Presently, at the age of 68 years old, Mr Koh is still going strong as a dedicated staff of the Singapore Examinations and Assessment Board. As he puts it: 'What I lack in education, I make up for it by dedication'.

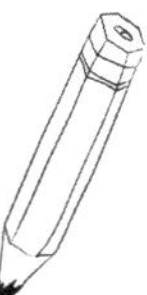

Mr Koh in the Examinations Branch, 1960s.

Mr Koh receiving the Public Service Administrative Medal (Silver) in 1964.

Mr Koh in the Singapore Examinations and Assessment Board, Exams Operations Department, 2008.

25 November 1961 — Combined Chinese Middle School Students Mass Rally at Chinese High School Bukit Timah Road to boycott the Singapore Government Chinese Secondary IV Examinations. (By courtesy of Singapore Press Holdings — *The Straits Times*.)

28 November 1961 — About 300 students picketed the three entrances to the emergency examination centre at the Ministry of Education at Kay Siang Road. (By courtesy of Singapore Press Holdings — *The Straits Times*.)

29 November 1961 — Student pickets outside the Teacher's Training College stop a Department of Social Services van at Paterson Road to plaster it with poster strips denouncing the change in the Singapore Chinese secondary education system. (By courtesy of Singapore Press Holdings — *The Straits Times*.)

29 November 1961 — A candidate for the Government Secondary IV Examination tried to enter the college emergency examination centre at Paterson Road by forcing his way through 'human chains' formed by rows of student pickets boycotting the examination. (By courtesy of Singapore Press Holdings — *The Straits Times*.)

OUTCOME OF THE EXAMINATION BOYCOTT

Given the tumultuous context of the examination boycott, MOE assured parents that the marking of the examination scripts would take into account the 'psychological handicaps' and 'unfavourable conditions' faced by candidates.[20] Supplementary examinations from 4 to 8 December were organised for candidates who had missed the examinations earlier. Three examination centres were set up at the Teachers Training College at Paterson Road and the Tanglin Boys' and Girls' Schools near MOE at Kay Siang Road.[21] In addition, the Government Senior Middle III Examination was held from 8 to 14 December 1961 at 44 examination centres, with no change in timetable or examination centres.[22]

5 December 1961 — Candidates taking the Elementary Mathematics Paper of the Supplementary Singapore Government Chinese Secondary IV Examination at the Teachers Training College centre hiding their faces from the camera. (By courtesy of Singapore Press Holdings — *The Straits Times*.)

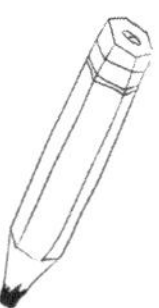

[20] *Legislative Assembly Debates State of Singapore*, Official Report, Third Session of the First Legislative Assembly, Part I of Third Session, from 31 October 1961 to 21 December 1961, Volume 15, Singapore: Government Printer, 1964, p. 1054.
[21] *The Straits Times*, 2 December 1961, p. 4.
[22] *Legislative Assembly Debates State of Singapore*, Official Report, Third Session of the First Legislative Assembly, Part I of Third Session, from 31 October 1961 to 21 December 1961, Volume 15, Singapore: Government Printer, 1964, p. 1055.

At the end of the week of boycott, the government would have considered the examination boycott a failure given that more than half of the candidates attended the examinations. Yet, at the end of the final day of examination boycott, defiant student pickets held a 'victory march' on the grounds of The Chinese High School.[23] Even during the supplementary examinations, there were pickets forming human chains to prevent students from entering examination rooms.[24] However, the pickets 'vanished' after the Legislative Assembly voted to authorise the government to provide police protection for parents and students.[25]

Mr Yong Nguk Lin, the then Minister of Education, gave an impassioned speech on the reasons for failure of the boycott in the Legislative Assembly on 1 December 1961:[26]

> The first reason is that the Government, in tackling this delicate issue, steadfastly refused to fall into the Communist trap of hitting out at the misguided and excited student picketers in order to get at the manipulators who hid behind the students and who in their cowardly way used the bodies of school children as their shield.
>
> …. The second reason is that…public opinion was on the side of the Government's stand which was that no one was compelled to take this examination…the vast majority of students wanted to take this examination…. If there had been no intimidation by hostile and unruly picketers, there is no doubt that the attendance would have been higher.
>
> …. The third reason…is that students and parents on their own initiative decided that they are not going to be cowed by the picketers and their cowardly leaders…. This should be a good lesson to the pro-Communist conspirators that the days are

[23] *The Straits Times*, 2 December 1961, p. 1.
[24] *Legislative Assembly Debates State of Singapore*, Official Report, in Third Session of the First Legislative Assembly, Part I of Third Session, from 31 October 1961 to 21 December 1961, Volume 15, Singapore: Government Printer, 1964, p. 1130.
[25] *The Straits Times*, 6 December 1961, p. 1.
[26] *Legislative Assembly Debates State of Singapore*, Official Report, in Third Session of the First Legislative Assembly, Part I of Third Session, from 31 October 1961 to 21 December 1961, Volume 15, Singapore: Government Printer, 1964, pp. 1056–1057.

gone when they could intimidate the people and bamboozle students and parents with false slogans.

.... The past week's events have shown that there is no real foundation for the myth that Chinese schools are centres of unrest and indiscipline.

The results of the 1961 Government Secondary IV Examination and Senior Middle III Examination were as follows: 2,100 out of 2,958 students sat for the Government Secondary IV Examination, with 77.85% passes; and 4,261 out of 4,308 students sat for the Senior Middle III Examination, with 62% passes.[27] The *MOE Annual Report 1961* commended the candidates and their parents for 'exercising their democratic right to sit an examination which they felt to be to their advantage'.[28]

1962 marked an end to the 'most glaring example of unequal treatment between English and Chinese secondary school leavers'.[29] The Government Senior Middle III Examination was held for the last time. Previously, this examination taken after a six-year course for the Chinese stream was equated to the Cambridge School Certificate taken after a four-year course for the English stream. With the Government Secondary IV Examination, secondary students in both the Chinese and English streams had the same duration of education and same recognition for government employment and teacher training.[30] Upper secondary classes were also introduced to enable students in the Chinese stream to proceed to higher education on the same terms as students in the English stream.[31]

AN EDUCATIONAL MEANS TO A POLITICAL END?

For the government, the examination boycott illustrated the challenges of forging a national education system. The educational issue was equal treatment for the two different education systems for the English and Chinese stream schools. Yet, for the activists of the boycott, the

[27] *Ministry of Education Annual Report 1961*, Singapore: Government Printing Office 1962, p. 6.
[28] Ibid., p. 5.
[29] *Ministry of Education Annual Report 1962*, Singapore: Government Printing Office, 1964, p. 1.
[30] Ibid.
[31] Ibid.

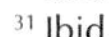

educational issue centred on the new requirement that would restrict access to higher education in Chinese. Previously, the only requirement for the Chinese stream students to progress to Senior Middle III was the need to pass the internal school examination. With the new 6-4-2 structure, if the students did not passed the Government Secondary IV Examination, they would not be able to proceed to the Government Upper Secondary II Examination. Some pickets from the 'boycott action committee' claimed that they were against the new requirement and had no connection with any political parties.[32] The Chinese community, however, was not unanimous in its views on this issue. Before the examinations, the education minister had an amicable resolution on the concerns raised by the Chinese Schools Committee-Teacher Association (regarded as the highest organisation of Chinese education in Singapore) and agreed to its request that students who passed the internal school examination but failed Government Secondary IV Examination could be promoted to upper secondary classes.[33] The principals of the secondary schools had also stood by the government's decision in the implementation of the new examinations. Most parents also supported the new examinations and escorted their children to the examination centres against all odds.

Yet, beyond purely educational concerns, the examination boycott represented an educational issue caught in the political battle for merger. The education minister argued that the cry of Chinese education being in danger was raised only after the merger issue came to the forefront.[34] In July 1961, the pro-communists and left-wing members of the People's Action Party (PAP) who were opposed to the terms of merger with Malaya had split from PAP to form a new political party, the Barisan Socialis. The Barisan Socialis had strong connections with Chinese trade and worker unions and Chinese middle school students. At the same time, the series of events that culminated in the examination boycott was clearly not the work of student pickets alone, but involved wider forces. In June 1961, the Chinese School Teachers' Union raised controversy over the examinations. The Nanyang Students' Union made a failed attempt to rally the monitors of all

---

[32] *The Straits Times*, 2 December 1961, p. 4.
[33] *Legislative Assembly Debates State of Singapore*, Official Report, in Third Session of the First Legislative Assembly, Part I of Third Session, from 31 October 1961 to 21 December 1961, Volume 15, Singapore: Government Printer, 1964, p. 772.
[34] Ibid., p. 767.

secondary schools at the Hokkien Association.[35] In November 1961, a Barisan Socialis publication gave publicity to student agitation and presented a distorted view of the education minister's interview with student delegation.[36] During the boycott, it was also observed that banners and posters supporting the boycott were prominently displayed on the buses of companies whose workers were connected to the Singapore Bus Workers' Union. It was also observed that a number of people connected to the Barisan Socialis were seen talking to the pickets during the examination boycott.[37] The student pickets also seemed very well-organised — there were plans by agitators 'to get into examination halls, tear up examination papers and force the examinees to disperse'.[38]

From the government's standpoint, the examination boycott was an issue that was exploited by the communists to achieve their political ends. According to the education minister, the communists cadres were manipulating Chinese schools 'to whip emotion' and spread 'widespread chaos and trouble in order to stem the rising tide of merger'.[39] Subsequently, a Commission of Inquiry was appointed to inquire into the examination boycott.

CONCLUSION

The impact of the examination boycott was both short and long term. In the short term, the Chinese examination boycott illustrated the challenges of forging a national examination system. It could be seen as either arising from purely educational concerns with the erosion of Chinese education, or characteristic of the politics of its times — the manipulation of Chinese students started by the communists and pro-communists in the 1950s and persisted till the beginning of the 1960s, amidst the political battle for merger. In the long term, the streamlining of the four language streams into a 6-4-2 system was a sensible approach to accord parity of treatment for all and laid the foundation for a national system of education and national unity in Singapore.

[35] Ibid., p. 72.
[36] Ibid., pp. 773–775.
[37] Ibid., p. 771.
[38] Ibid., p. 767.
[39] Ibid., pp. 765–766.

Charting Our Destiny

(1980s – 2007)

tonnes of soybean and maize imported
of that time approximately 2% GM
to take both the industry and
level by surprise. There was no
GM foods and there was no agreement
GM and non-GM produce.
of the European food industry did
non-GM soybeans in particular. The
premium price soybeans from crops that had
and they could keep the non-GM produce
supply chain. Nevertheless, they could not
absolutely no mixing of GM and non-GM
pay the asking price anyway.
processors turned to Brazil for a supply of
that supply is unlikely to last much longer
herbicide-tolerant GM soybeans into Brazil. In the
choice between labeling all products

CHAPTER

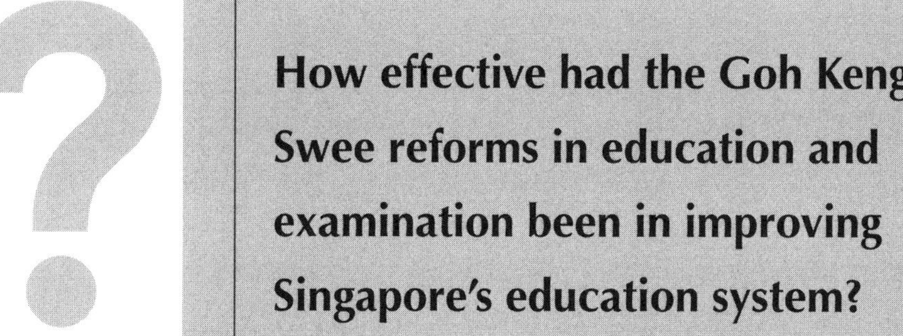
How effective had the Goh Keng
Swee reforms in education and
examination been in improving
Singapore's education system?

It has not occurred to many Singaporeans how unnatural the present school system is…. Our system is largely modelled on the British pattern but the societal and demographic background could hardly be more dissimilar. If as a result of a world calamity, children in England were taught Russian and Mandarin, while they continue to speak English at home, the British education system would run into some of the problems which have been plaguing the schools in Singapore and the Ministry of Education.[1]

Report on the Ministry of Education (1978)

In 1978, Dr Goh Keng Swee, the then Deputy Prime Minister, led a study team to identify the problems in Singapore's education system. The team's recommendations, as outlined in the *Report on the Ministry of Education (MOE)*, had far-reaching ramifications on Singapore's education system up till today. Three major shortcomings in the education system were identified, namely high educational wastage, low levels of literacy and ineffective bilingualism.[2]

The study team found that attrition rates in Singapore's education system (29% at primary level and 36% at secondary level) were very much higher than the comparison systems (Taiwan, Japan, the United Kingdom [UK] and France). Based on the examination results, the team

---

[1] Goh Keng Swee, *Report on the Ministry of Education, 1978*, Singapore: Ministry of Education, 10 February 1979, p. 1–1.
[2] Ibid., p. 4–1.

also found that less than 40% of the pupil population passed both their first and second language examinations. A Ministry of Defence survey among English-educated national servicemen showed that only 11% were able to handle well in situations where the English language was the sole means of communication.[3]

This unsatisfactory state of affairs could be attributed to a number of factors. Firstly, the existing education system was a rigid one, with all schools following a common curriculum and examinations, regardless of differences in pupil abilities. Moreover, the GCE O-Level examination, which was designed for a five-year secondary education (in the UK), was completed over four years in Singapore. Secondly, as part of the efforts to emphasise bilingualism, the exposure time allocated to English as a second language in non-English stream schools had increased over the years and this contributed to increased workload for pupils. Finally, the promotion and retention policy also allowed students to be promoted automatically to the next level irrespective of their ability to cope with the higher demands at both primary and secondary levels.

THE 1978 REFORMS

Having identified the problems of the education system and their underlying causes, the study team proposed several key recommendations which were subsequently implemented. These recommendations created a system of ability-based streaming where students were streamed to different courses according to their ability. The intent was to 'provide an opportunity for the less capable pupils to develop at a pace slower than that for the more capable pupils'.[4] Consequently, differentiated examinations were provided for the different courses.

Primary Education

In 1980, the New Education System (NES) was implemented at the primary level. It created different ability streams for the primary course:

[3] Ibid., pp. 3–5, 3–7 & 3–8.
[4] Ibid., p. 6–10.

Normal Bilingual, Extended Bilingual and Monolingual. Based on the results of end-of-year Primary 3 streaming examination, pupils were channelled into the three different ability streams:

(a) In the Normal Bilingual stream, pupils would learn two languages (English and Mother Tongue) and take the PSLE at the end of Primary 6.

(b) In the Extended Bilingual stream, pupils would take the PSLE at the end of Primary 8, so that they could benefit from a bilingual education but at a slower pace.

(c) In the Monolingual stream, pupils would sit for a different examination, the Primary School Proficiency Examination (PSPE), at the end of Primary 8. These pupils who were not academically inclined and could not cope with the learning of two languages, would instead focus on language and basic numeracy to prepare them for vocational training at the Vocational and Industrial Training Board (VITB).

To allow for late developers, provision was made for lateral movements across the three streams.

In the area of assessment, the Goh Keng Swee reforms brought about the following key changes. One, the Primary 3 streaming examination was introduced. Pupils were assessed in English Language, Mathematics and Mother Tongue Language, so that parents could be guided on the stream best suited for their children. To minimise the potentially stressful effect of a national examination at this level, a school-based assessment system based on an item bank was put in place. This was a key innovation, as it allowed schools to design examination papers to suit their students' profile and yet maintain a measure of comparability across schools. In this assessment system, MOE developed test items that were then calibrated in terms of difficulty level. Schools would design their examination papers by selecting test items from the item bank but adhering to specified parameters such as the overall difficulty level of the paper. In this way, there was some degree of customisation at the school level whilst maintaining comparability of standards across schools.

Two, at the end of primary education, there was a new examination, the PSPE, in addition to the PSLE.[5] The PSPE, intended for pupils in the Monolingual stream, assessed their basic literacy and numeracy skills and hence their readiness for further education and training at VITB. The PSLE was meant for pupils in the Normal Bilingual and Extended Bilingual streams, who would be examined in English Language, Mother Tongue, Mathematics and Science. The PSLE would serve three purposes: to certify the level of achievement of students in each subject; determine the secondary school stream for students; and post students to secondary schools based on merit.

Secondary Education

The recommendations of the study team were translated into the NES at secondary level. It created different ability streams for the secondary course: Special Bilingual, Express and Normal. Based on the PSLE results, the students would be posted to the three different streams:

(a) In the Special Bilingual stream, students would offer both English and Chinese at first language level and sit for the GCE O-Level examination at the end of Secondary 4.

(b) In the Express stream, students would offer English at first language level and Mother Tongue at second language level and like the Special Bilingual students, sit for the O-Level examination at the end of Secondary 4.

(c) In the Normal stream, students would offer a reduced curriculum which is a sub-set of the O-Level curriculum. They would sit for the GCE Normal-Level (N-Level) examination at the end of Secondary 4. If they do well in this examination, they will proceed to a fifth year and offer the O-Level examination.

As in the NES for primary level, provision was made for students to move across streams at the secondary level, depending on their performance. Furthermore, with the introduction of the GCE N-

---

[5] The PSPE was conducted from 1984 to 1992.

Level examination in 1984, a differentiated examination system was established for secondary schools, with the O-Level catering to students from the Special and Express streams and the N-Level to those from the Normal stream.

IMPACT OF THE REFORMS

The Goh Keng Swee reforms resulted in a differentiated education system which recognised that not all students can benefit from a 'one size fits all' approach. Instead, different curricula and different examinations could cater to the differing abilities and learning needs of students.

The reforms also addressed the difficulties faced by some students in the learning of English Language and their Mother Tongue language. Thus, at the secondary level, students could offer their Mother Tongue language at three levels — as a first language at O-Level for those in the Special stream, as a second language at O-Level for those in the Express stream and as a second language at N-Level for those in the Normal stream.

However, the Goh Keng Swee reforms were not without its critics. Some critics felt that streaming at Primary 3 was too early and did not provide opportunities for late developers. Other critics regarded streaming as elitist and highlighted the stigmatisation effect of labelling students. These criticisms notwithstanding, after 12 to 15 years of implementation, the Goh Keng Swee reforms produced some positive results.

Reducing Education Wastage

One of the key findings of the study team was the high attrition rate in Singapore. In 1980, before streaming was introduced, only 58% of a Primary 1 cohort completed secondary school. By 2000, the proportion was 93%.[6] There was also an improvement in student achievement, as measured by examination results. In 1981, only 40%

[6] Ministry of Education, FY2001 Committee of Supply Debate, 15 March 2001, Minister's First Reply on Schools, "Making an ability driven education happen".

of a Primary 1 cohort passed in at least three O-Level subjects. This went up to 65% of a cohort 10 years later.[7]

International Comparisons

Improved student achievement showed up in the results of Singapore students in international comparisons of educational achievement. In the Second International Science Study conducted by the International Association for the Evaluation of Educational Achievement (IEA) in 1982, Singapore students were ranked 16th out of 26 participating countries in science achievement. A decade later, in IEA's *Trends in Mathematics and Science Study* (TIMSS) of 1993, Singapore students outperformed students from all 45 participating countries in Mathematics at Grades 3, 4, 7 and 8. In Science, Singapore was ranked first for students at Grades 7 and 8 (Secondary 1 and 2) and seventh at Grades 3 and 4 (Primary 3 and 4).

Subsequent studies of TIMSS confirmed the high level of achievement of Singapore students in Mathematics and Science. By the 2003 TIMSS, Singapore students ranked first in both Mathematics and Science at Grades 4 (Primary 4) and 8 (Secondary 2).

The significant improvement in student achievement is not confined to Mathematics and Science. In the 2001 *Progress in Reading Literacy Study* (PIRLS), Singapore students showed a high level of reading achievement. In PIRLS, Grade 4 students are normally assessed in their Mother Tongue (thus, students in Sweden were assessed by reading texts in Swedish). Singapore was the sole exception in that our students were assessed in the English language and not their Mother Tongue languages. Among 35 countries, Singapore came in 15th with an average score equal to that of Scotland and just one point behind New Zealand.

Five years later, in the 2006 PIRLS, the performance of Singapore students improved significantly over the 2001 study and ranked 4th out of 20 countries. Moreover, Singapore outperformed all other countries

---

[7] *Improving Primary School Education*, Report of the Review Committee, Ministry of Education, March 1991, p. 1.

which assessed students solely in the English language, i.e., the US, England, Scotland, as well as Trinidad and Tobago.

CONCLUSION

By all measures, the reforms introduced by Dr Goh Keng Swee and implemented over a comparatively short period of 15 years resulted in an education system envied by many — a very low attrition rate and very high average achievement. This phase of education reforms was to be termed an 'efficiency-driven' education system later. The 1978 reforms contributed significantly to Singapore's efforts to develop its human capital and produced a highly skilled and productive workforce, providing Singapore with a strong foundation to face new challenges in an increasingly competitive and globalised world.

CHAPTER

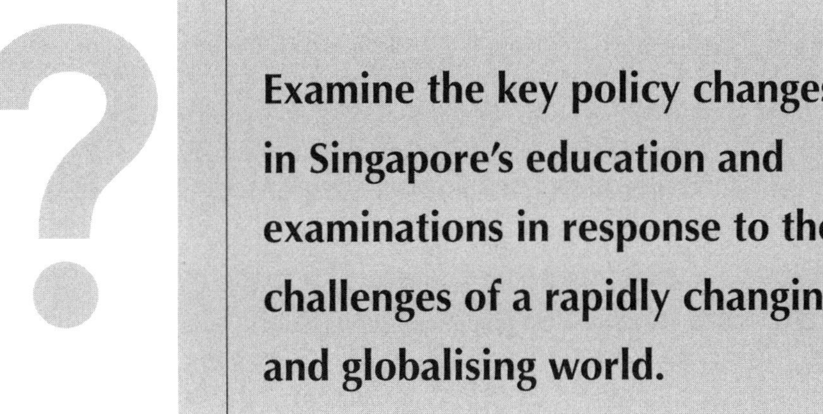

Examine the key policy changes in Singapore's education and examinations in response to the challenges of a rapidly changing and globalising world.

Our future will depend on our ability to grasp new concepts; learn and adapt throughout life; and create and innovate. And so too our schools to prepare our children for tomorrow.[1]

Teo Chee Hean
the then Minister for Education
Speech at 2002 MOE Workplan Seminar

The Goh Keng Swee reforms aimed at addressing the 'efficiency' of the education system — reducing attrition and raising achievement. On both counts, the reforms had achieved the desired outcomes. By the turn of the century, the Singapore education system achieved international recognition as one of very high standards, particularly in Mathematics and Science.

With the emergence of a national system of education, a low attrition rate and high achievement in Mathematics and Science, the Ministry of Education (MOE) undertook a series of reviews and reforms to ensure that the Singapore education system continue to meet the needs of the future, in a rapidly changing and globalising world.

THE 1991 REFORMS — IMPROVING PRIMARY SCHOOL EDUCATION

In 1990, the then Minister of Education, Dr Tony Tan appointed Mr John Yip, then Director of Education, to review primary school education and recommend measures for the improvement of the system for the 1990s and beyond.[2] The Committee's report, *Improving Primary Education*

---

[1] Speech by RAdm Teo Chee Hean, Minister for Education and Second Minister for Defence at the MOE Workplan Seminar, 18 September 2002.

[2] *Improving Primary Education*, Report of Review Committee, March 1991.

tabled at the March 1991 Schools Council meeting, identified three areas requiring attention:

(a) the need to provide all pupils with an adequate grounding in English Language and Mathematics, particularly among the least able, so that they could benefit from further education and training;

(b) whether the streaming of pupils at the end of Primary 3 was too early; and

(c) the poor image of post-primary vocational education and training.

The Committee's recommendations were accepted and implemented. Streaming was postponed to Primary 4 and all primary pupils would have six years of primary education and take a modified PSLE. Streaming at the end of Primary 4 would place pupils in one of the three language streams. Pupils in all streams would learn English Language as a first language and Mother Tongue at one of three levels — as a first language (EM1 stream), as a second language (EM2 stream) and at an oral proficiency level (EM3 stream). In the modified PSLE, pupils in all streams would offer common English Language and Mathematics papers but different Mother Tongue Language papers. In addition, pupils in the EM3 stream did not offer Science. With the introduction of the modified PSLE in 1993, the Primary School Proficiency Examination for the Monolingual stream was abolished.

The Committee's reforms meant that pupils who passed the PSLE would proceed to secondary school for a further four to five years of schooling. Thus, all pupils would receive at least 10 years of general education before proceeding to various post-secondary institutions. Previously, pupils in the Monolingual stream would proceed for pre-vocational education and training at the Vocational and Industrial Training Board's (VITB) institutes.

As a consequence of the 1991 reforms in primary education, appropriate modifications were also made at the secondary and post-secondary education.[3] To cater to the less academically inclined, a new course

---

[3] *The Education System (1991): Implementation Guidelines Secondary Schools*, Schools Division, Ministry of Education, August 1993.

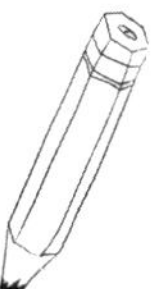

was introduced at the secondary level: the Normal (Technical) or
N(T) course. Students in both the Normal (Academic), or N(A), and
the N(T) courses would offer the GCE N-Level examination at the
end of 4 years. In 1997, the first cohort of the N(T) course took the
N-Level examination.[4] Upon completion of the N-Level examination,
the students proceeded to the Institute of Technical Education (which
had replaced the VITB) or join the workforce.

The N(T) course was designed to strengthen pupils' proficiency in
English and Mathematics and prepare them for technical-vocational
education and training at the post-secondary level. The N(T) course
introduced further differentiation in the type of examinations available
for pupils of different abilities. The curriculum included more technical-
vocational types of subjects such as Computer Applications and
Elements of Office Administration. In both subjects, pupils were assessed
on their information technology skills using computers. These new
subjects called for different ways of assessing pupil achievement.

While the N(T) course worked well, the English Language and
Mathematics papers in the modified PSLE proved to be too difficult for
pupils in the EM3 stream. In 1996, further differentiation was introduced
at the PSLE to cater to these pupils. Instead of taking the common
English Language and Mathematics papers, two new subjects were
introduced, namely Foundation English and Foundation Mathematics,
to meet the abilities and needs of pupils in the EM3 stream.

The setting up of the Institute of Technical Education (ITE) was a key
component of the 1991 reforms. Prior to this, the VITB was responsible
for the provision of vocational education. Unfortunately, VITB was
not well regarded and was perceived to be a place for failures. VITB
admitted a wide range of students, from those with O-Levels to
those who did not pass the PSLE. With the 1991 reforms, VITB was
reconstituted as ITE and positioned as a post-secondary educational
institution. Over the years, ITE has transformed itself dramatically,
from being labelled 'It's The End' in the Singapore-made film, *I Not
Stupid*, to a global leader in technical education. Its many accolades
include the Global IBM Innovations Award in Transforming Government,

---

[4] Elaine P. Y. Lim & Annie Tan, "Education assessment in Singapore", in *Assessment in Education*,
Vol. 6, No. 3, 1999, p. 397.

administered by Harvard University's Ash Institute for Democratic Governance and Innovation (2007) and the Singapore Quality Award for World-Class Business Excellence (2005).[5]

MOULDING THE FUTURE OF THE NATION — THINKING SCHOOLS, LEARNING NATION

The 1991 reforms marked the beginnings of Singapore's efforts to prepare pupils for a rapidly changing world, characterised by technological advances, the explosion of information and increasing economic competitiveness in a globalised world. To ensure that pupils are 'future-ready', it was no longer sufficient for them to be armed with factual knowledge. The ability to apply knowledge and to be creative and innovative became increasingly the more important facets of education.

At the turn of the century, the 'Thinking Schools, Learning Nations' (TSLN) vision of 1997 set the context for a further review of the education system. TSLN envisaged Singapore as a nation of thinking and committed citizens capable of meeting the challenges of the future, and an education system geared to the needs of the 21st century. MOE undertook a fundamental review of the education system to develop in students creative thinking and learning skills for the future, to utilise information technology more widely and to develop communication skills and habits of independent learning. National education was also strengthened to develop stronger bonds between students and a desire to contribute to something larger than themselves.[6] Curriculum and assessment moved in tandem with this vision. Thinking skills were infused in the curriculum, while there was a gradual shift in examinations to a better balance between assessing recall of factual information and higher order thinking skills such as application of concepts. At the secondary level, a compulsory subject, Combined Humanities, was introduced. In the Social Studies component of Combined Humanities, elements of National Education were included.

---

[5] *Key Milestones in ITE's Transformation (1992 to 2007)*, http://www.ite.edu.sg/about_ite/milestones.htm

[6] "Shaping our future: Thinking Schools, Learning Nation", Speech by Prime Minister Goh Chok Tong at the Opening of the 7th International Conference on Thinking, 2 June 1997.

Alternative Modes of Assessment

Another important development in national examinations was the introduction of alternative modes of assessment. In the 1950s and 1960s, most examinations were pen-and-paper-based, with the exception of subjects like Science, which had a practical component. Subsequently, the introduction of more subjects involving practical components and the need for students to learn more skills saw the need for alternative modes of assessment. Recognising the limitations of pen-and-paper-based assessment, examinations in Singapore included alternative modes which were more suited to the learning outcomes of various subjects.

In 1984, the first listening comprehension examination was conducted for N-Level English Language. In this examination, students listened to an audio stimulus such as an announcement at an event and answered questions based on what they had heard. As it was difficult to produce cassette tapes of consistent quality under secure conditions, a bold innovation was introduced. The listening comprehension audio stimuli was broadcasted 'live' over radio! Measures were taken to equip schools with good radio sets and various tests were conducted to ensure good reception of radio signals. Arrangements were also made to minimise noise near examination centres. Today, listening comprehension remains an important component in most of our language examinations.

The move towards more authentic assessment also saw the introduction of coursework in many subjects such as Design and Technology, Computer Applications and Elements of Office Administration. The coursework assessment is school-based and spread over a period of time, as opposed to a time-based pen-and-paper examination.

As MOE gained more confidence in coursework and school-based assessment, more innovations were introduced. A major innovation was Project Work at A-Level. Project Work was a key recommendation of the Committee on University Admission set up in 1999. The aim of Project Work was to provide pre-university students with opportunities to explore the inter-relationships and inter-connectedness of subject-specific knowledge. Project Work was a learning experience which aimed to provide students with the opportunity to synthesise knowledge from various areas of learning and critically and creatively apply it to real-life situations. The students had to demonstrate their ability individually and as a group, by applying knowledge learnt to develop a project task. This process enhanced students' knowledge and enabled them to acquire skills like collaboration, communication and independent learning. In so doing, Project Work would prepare students for lifelong learning and the future ahead.[7] Project Work was trialled in 2001, underwent a dry-run in 2002 and was examined for the first time in 2003.

JUNIOR COLLEGE AND UPPER SECONDARY EDUCATION REVIEW

In 2002, Minister of Education Teo Chee Hean appointed the then Senior Minister of State for Trade & Industry and Education, Mr Tharman Shanmugaratnam, to chair a committee to review junior college (JC) and upper secondary education with the view of ensuring that education in Singapore remained relevant in a knowledge-based economy. The committee recommended 'diversity and flexibility' as the way forward. The committee's recommendations that had a major impact on examinations were a broader and more flexible JC curriculum; and a more diverse JC/upper secondary education landscape.[8]

The Revised JC Curriculum

The revised JC curriculum aimed to nurture students' thinking and communication skills, provide greater flexibility to better cater to students' strengths and interests and a broad-based curriculum that emphasised the inter-connections between disciplines. This curriculum resulted in a radical change in the GCE A-Level examination that had remained largely unchanged since 1975, when it replaced the Cambridge Higher School Certificate.

The key changes for the revised A-Level examination, first examined in November 2007, were as follows:[9]

---

[7] *Project Work Examination Syllabus*, Singapore: Ministry of Education, 2007, pp. 1–2.
[8] *Report of the Junior College/Upper Secondary Review Committee*, Ministry of Education, 2002, pp. i–ii.
[9] Ibid., p. 12.

- The new A-Level examinations were offered at three levels of study, Higher 1 (H1), Higher 2 (H2) and Higher 3 (H3), replacing the previous system of AO, A and S (Special) papers. Candidates could now have more flexibility in offering content subjects at either H1 and H2 levels;

- H1 subjects were half of H2 in breadth of content but similar to H2 in depth of rigour;

- H2 subjects were equivalent in demand and rigour to the previous A-Level subjects;

- The H3 subjects, building on the corresponding H2 subjects, provided opportunities for students to achieve peaks of excellence within the context of broad-based education and for new and more independent modes of learning and exploration;

- Subjects would be grouped into broad disciplines, such as Knowledge Skills (General Paper, Project Work and Knowledge and Inquiry), Languages, Humanities & the Arts, and Mathematics and Science;

- To provide a broader education, students would have to offer a contrasting subject, that is, a subject outside their main areas of specialisation. Thus, a student who offered mostly Science subjects would need to take at least one subject from the Humanities & the Arts group; and

- General Paper, Project Work and Mother Tongue Language would be compulsory subjects.

These changes represented a major departure from the existing A-Level examination. One significant innovation was that, instead of a subject examination in which students could offer any combination of subjects within a course, the revised A-Level examination required students to offer a contrasting subject.

The other significant innovation was the different modes of H3 subjects. In addition to the traditional pen-and-paper examination, H3 subjects could also take the form of an extended, in-depth research essay, or a university undergraduate course module. A number of these subjects are developed in collaboration with MOE partners, including the National University of Singapore (NUS), Nanyang Technological University (NTU), Singapore Management University (SMU) and the Agency for Science, Technology and Research (A*STAR). Thus, students would have a wider option of programmes offered by different educational institutions to cater to their ability and interests. In the 2007 examination, there were 13 subjects offered by MOE, and 17 subjects offered by MOE partners, in various modes.

The revised A-Level examination provided for greater flexibility and choice for students, whilst giving greater focus on knowledge skills. In 2005, a survey conducted by Cambridge International Examinations showed strong endorsement for the revised A-Level curriculum and examination from leading universities in the United Kindom (UK), the United States (US), Australia, Canada and New Zealand, as seen from comments below:[10]

> LSE welcomes several aspects of the new curriculum. The requirement to study a contrasting subject at H1 or H2 level will ensure students follow the multi-disciplinary approach required for admission to many LSE courses. The opportunity for students to take an additional study at H3 level will also enable admissions tutors to identify high ability candidates in, for example, Mathematics. It is also pleasing to see the inclusion of thinking and communication skills in the core curriculum.
>
> — London School of Economics and Political Science

> The new curriculum and qualifications framework build on the academic strengths and subject specialization of the present system. The various core curriculum elements, which are consistent with the qualities and skills which Princeton seeks to promote, are also welcomed as an enhancement. Therefore, we look forward in future years to applications from students in Singapore who have studied within the new curriculum.
>
> — Princeton University

[10] *Final Report on Singapore-Cambridge Curriculum and Qualifications Framework Recognition Project,* November 2005.

A MORE DIVERSE EDUCATION LANDSCAPE

International studies such as the *Trends in Mathematics and Science Study* (TIMSS) showed that Singapore's students attained high averages in Mathematics and Science. For example, in the 2003 TIMSS study, 44% of Singapore's students attained the 'Advanced International Benchmark' in Mathematics, compared to 7% internationally. While this was a notable achievement, an important question was whether the education system was too constraining on the most able.

The review committee noted that there was no single formula for preparing Singapore's young for an innovation-driven and fast-changing future and recommended that Singapore move towards a more diverse education system that would better cater to the different interests and talents of its students. To this end, greater diversity was introduced in the education system.

In 2004, the introduction of the Integrated Programme (IP) enabled secondary school students in selected schools to proceed to JCs without taking the O-Level examinations.[11] The IP provided students who are clearly university-bound the opportunity to engage in a broader learning experience and a seamless upper secondary and JC education,[12] instead of having to prepare for two major examinations (i.e., the O-Level and A-Level) in a span of four years. At the end of IP, students could offer the A-Level examination or the International Baccaulaureate (IB) depending on which school they enrolled in. In 2004, the Raffles and Hwa Chong families of schools, National Junior College and Anglo-Chinese School (Independent) became IP Schools.

In addition, specialised independent schools were also set up, namely the Singapore Sports School, the National University of Singapore High School for Mathematics and Science and the School of the Arts Singapore. These schools were intended to add greater diversity and choice in the Singapore education system.

---

[11] *MOE Approves the Introduction of Integrated Programmes in Four Schools*, MOE Press Release, 30 December 2002.
[12] Ibid.

GREATER FLEXIBILITY AND CHOICE

A number of steps were also taken to provide greater flexibility and choice within the primary and secondary schools. Consequently, national examinations had to adjust and cater to the introduction of new initiatives such subject-based banding, direct school admission for pupils progressing to secondary and post-secondary levels and an expanded range of subjects for examinations at the secondary level.

Subject-Based Banding in Primary Schools

As part of the move to allow pupils and parents greater choice and decisions, subject-based banding would be introduced from 2008 for the Primary 5 cohort. Prior to this, the EM1 and EM2 streams had been merged in 2004, and schools were given flexibility to develop their own year-end Primary 4 examination for the purpose of identifying pupils for different streams at Primary 5. With subject-based banding, pupils could offer a mix of Standard or Foundation subjects depending on their aptitude in each subject. The Standard subjects would be higher in demand and rigour compared to the Foundation subjects. This would benefit pupils who are in the merged stream (EM1 and 2), but had difficulties coping with some subjects at the Standard level, or pupils in the EM3 stream who had specific strengths in one or two subjects at the Standard level.[13]

Direct School Admission (DSA)

The DSA allowed for broader consideration of both academic and non-academic merits beyond performance in national examinations for placement in secondary schools, JCs and polytechnics. Consequently, whilst the PSLE and O-Level examinations would still be the major deciding factor for placement of students at the next stage of education, secondary schools and post-secondary institutions would have greater autonomy in the admission of students. DSA also provided students more pathways for progression in education based on their talents and interests.

[13] *Refining How We Deliver Ability Driven Education*, MOE Press Release, 28 September 2006.

From 2006 onwards, Autonomous and Independent secondary schools could offer up to 10% and 20% of their Secondary 1 enrolment for DSA. DSA was also extended to other mainstream secondary schools that were able to develop niches of excellence, for up to 5% of their Secondary 1 enrolment.[14] In addition, JCs not offering the IP were given the discretion to admit up to 10% of their intake based on their own criteria under the DSA.[15] From 2007 onwards, the Direct Polytechnic Admission (DPA) exercise allowed students who were intent on an applied education pathway to receive confirmed places in the polytechnics prior to taking their O-Level examinations.[16]

Expanding the Range of Subjects in Examinations

The range of subjects for national examinations was also broadened to allow for greater flexibility and choice.

From 2005, secondary schools could develop or build upon their existing niche areas by offering new O-Level subjects in addition to, or as replacement of current curriculum offerings.[17] They could explore syllabuses offered by the University of Cambridge Local Examinations Syndicate (UCLES), ranging from subjects in the International General Certificate of Secondary Education (IGCSE) or the OCR[18] General Certificate of Secondary Education (GCSE) subjects.

From 2006, selected students in the N(T) course could offer up to two N(A) subjects from the whole suite of N(A) subjects while selected students in the N(A) course could offer up to two O-Level subjects from an expanded range of subjects.[19]

From 2008 onwards, selected secondary schools would also be able to offer new O-Level subjects in applied disciplines (collectively

[14] *Greater Flexibility in the School Admission System*, MOE Press Release, 17 March 2004.

[15] Ibid. and *Direct School Admission Exercise 2005 for JC1 and Equivalent Level*, MOE Press Release, 9 May 2005.

[16] *Enriching Our Curriculum: Expanding Applied Learning Options*, MOE Press Release, 7 March 2006.

[17] *New 'O' Level Subjects: A Handbook*. Singapore: Ministry of Education, Curriculum Planning and Development Division, 2005, p. 1.

[18] Oxford, Cambridge and Royal Society for the Arts (OCR) is responsible for GCSE examinations in the UK and is part of UCLES.

[19] *Review of the Normal (Technical) Course*, MOE Press Release, 29 September 2004 and *Expansion of Range of 'O' Level Subjects Open to Normal (Academic) Students*, MOE Press Release, 29 September 2004.

termed Applied Subjects) to provide more opportunities for students to pursue their interest in applied learning. Applied Subjects were jointly developed by these schools and polytechnics, and will be assessed and awarded by the partner polytechnic. These subjects would be offered by Express and N(A) students taking the O-Level examination and would be of comparable rigour to the Singapore-Cambridge GCE O-Level subjects. Achievement in these subjects would be recorded on the O-Level examination certificate.

GREATER CONTROL OF EXAMINATIONS

For many years, the GCE examinations (and its predecessors, the School Certificate and the Higher School Certificate) were 'external' examinations in the sense that the syllabuses, question papers and standards set were determined by UCLES. In the early years of Cambridge examinations, the syllabuses prescribed for UK schools were adopted in toto and examinations were November versions of the main examinations in the UK held in June. As noted earlier, these examinations were Anglo-centric and parts of the syllabuses were not always relevant to Singapore.

By the 1960s, however, there was a shift to localise certain syllabuses, for example, Geography and History, and a different set of examination papers were available for students in Singapore. The pace of localisation quickened in the 1990s as the education system geared itself to prepare students for new challenges.

In 2002, MOE assumed greater control of the GCE A-Level examination, in terms of responsibility over the development of the examination syllabuses, format of examination question papers, setting of standards and award of grades for all subjects offered.[20] In 2006, this new mode of collaboration was extended to the GCE O-Level examination. With Singapore taking greater control of these examinations, the syllabuses, question papers and standards set are no longer linked to UK's GCE examinations, or UCLES's international versions of the GCE examinations. In order that syllabuses and new emphases be reflected

---

[20] *MOE to Assume Greater Control over the GCE A-Level Examination in 2002*, MOE Press Release, 2 October 2000.

in examinations in a timely manner, it was essential for MOE to have greater autonomy, so as to customise the examinations to meet the needs of Singapore. The establishment of the Singapore Examinations and Assessment Board was a step in this direction.

CONCLUSION

The recent reforms introduced by MOE were aimed at creating a more diverse educational landscape with greater flexibility and choice for students. These reforms signalled the end of a 'one size fits all' education system, so that students could develop their talents and abilities in different areas. As Minister of Education, Mr Tharman Shanmugaratnam puts it:[21]

> There is no easy formula, and certainly no single way, of preparing our young for (the) future. If we educate our children in a narrow domain, for example by focusing too closely on maximizing their examination scores, we will be preventing them from making the most of the opportunities they will face when they leave the system. The best preparation we can give our young is a balanced and well-rounded education, helping them develop the range of essential skills and the strength of character that will enable them to adapt and thrive in an uncertain and rapidly changing environment. We have to provide them a diversity of options and they progress through the system, and help them discover different interests and talents in themselves. We have to nurture the curiosity in all our children, and give them the confidence and space to pursue their passions.

> If we do this well, we will help our young be ready for the future. As a society, we will achieve new peaks of excellence in different fields of endeavour and a robust citizenry. We will be a vibrant and dynamic nation.

[21] Speech by Mr Tharman Shanmugaratnam, Acting Minister for Education, at the appointment ceremony for principals, 30 December 2003.

CHAPTER

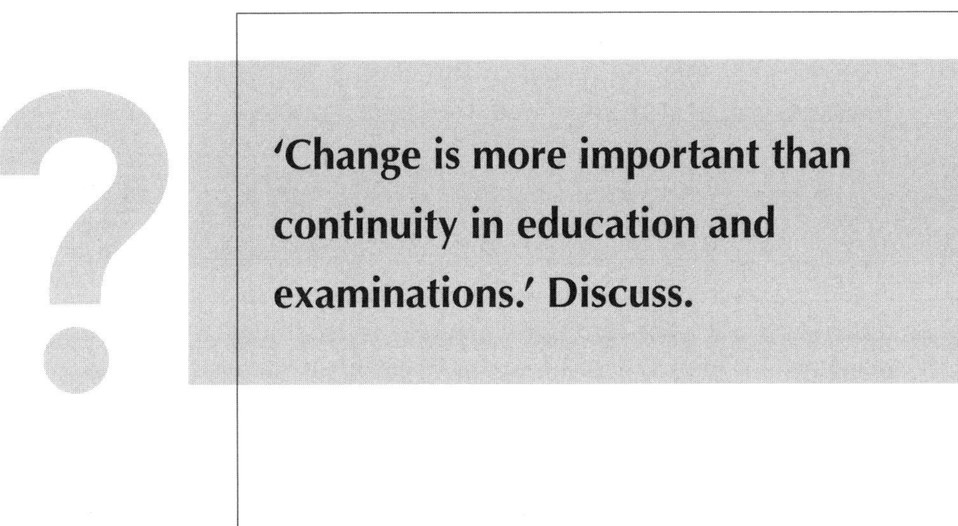

'Change is more important than continuity in education and examinations.' Discuss.

The preceding chapters surveyed the examinations landscape from the colonial days to the present, and how examinations have evolved in response to the requirements of an education system shaped by the changing contexts of politics, economy and society.

CHANGE

Education has undergone tremendous change, from the colonial era when Singapore was a British trading outpost to today's city-state. In the 1800s, the starting point was a hodgepodge of schools, curricula and examinations, reflecting the British colonial government's priorities and the sectoral interests of various communities. The disparate educational systems of English, Malay, Chinese and Tamil streams persisted until it was interrupted by the arrival of the Japanese invaders. From 1942 to 1945, the Japanese attempted to impose a common system based on the learning of the Japanese language and technical skills, but these attempts proved to be short-lived. The defeat of the Japanese and the return of the British led to the re-establishment of pre-war practices of language-based schools and examinations. Continuity triumphed over change, as there were no compelling reasons for change. The seeds of an English-medium education system and examination were planted with the setting up of an examination centre by the University of Cambridge Local Examinations Syndicate (UCLES), and the use of English as the language of instruction took root in post-war independent Singapore.

In 1959, when Singapore attained self-government, the government put in practice its pledge to accord equal treatment for the four language streams of education. Education and examination changed accordingly, with the establishment of four parallel streams, a common curriculum and four versions of the School Certificate Examination. These changes were consistent with the government's attempt to forge a common identity among the various communities in Singapore. Consequently, a process of 'standardisation' was set in motion.

Yet another change in education and examination was the emphasis on the learning of Science, Mathematics and Technical subjects. This change in curricula emphasis was in line with the need to create employment and provide sufficient trained manpower to support Singapore's rapid industrialisation programme.

The establishment of four equal language streams was an improvement from the disparate educational systems during the colonial era. In 1960, a common Primary School Leaving Examination (PSLE) was established at the end of primary schooling, albeit in different language streams. A common 6-4-2 system was well established at the end of secondary schooling, despite the 1961 boycott of the Government Secondary IV School Certificate (Chinese) Examination. In the 1960s, students from different language streams could qualify for common certificates — the School Certificate and Higher School Certificate examinations at the end of four years of secondary education and two years of pre-university education respectively. By the 1970s, the Singapore-Cambridge General Certificate of Education (GCE) Ordinary Level (O-Level) and Advanced Level (A-Level) examinations emerged as national certificates of educational attainment, reflecting the parity of four streams and similarity of academic standards.

While equal treatment was achieved for the four language streams, the better job prospects of an English stream education invariably proved to be a magnet for parents and students. Enrolment quickly shifted away from the Chinese, Malay and Tamil streams. By the mid-1980s, only one language stream survived — the English stream.

The Goh Keng Swee reforms of 1978 brought about further changes in the education landscape — setting in motion a process of differentiation. This time, it was prompted by high education wastage, ineffective bilingualism and low achievement. A 'one size fits all' approach to education and examination did not work well as it did not take into account differences in student ability. The 1978 reforms brought about several significant changes — the introduction of different courses to match the different pace of learning among different students. The common set of examinations gave way to different examinations, such as the Primary School Proficiency Examination (PSPE) for pupils in the Primary Monolingual course, and the GCE Normal Level (N-Level) examination for students in the secondary Normal course.

Notwithstanding the significant reduction in education wastage, further changes were made to the education system to make it more relevant to the needs of the 1990s. These changes were intended to help the less able students benefit more from education by giving them the opportunities to have at least 10 years of general education and preparing them better for post-secondary education and training programmes. The PSPE was scrapped and modifications were made to the PSLE, which became a placement examination. These changes provided all primary school pupils the opportunity of at least four years of secondary education before moving on to post-secondary education and training institutions. The Normal (Technical) or N(T) course was introduced and in 1997, the N-Level examination was conducted for the N(T) candidates for the first time.

At the turn of the century, the reforms of the 1980s and 1990s began to show results. Attrition was reduced to about 3% while students topped international surveys of achievement in Mathematics and Science. Yet another series of change was to emerge. According to Minister of Education, Mr Tharman Shanmugaratnam:[1]

> The best preparation we can give our young is a balanced and well-rounded education, helping them develop the range of essential skills and the strength of character that will enable them to adapt and thrive in an uncertain and rapidly changing environment. We have to provide them a diversity of options and they progress through the system, and help them discover different interests and talents in themselves. We have to nurture the curiosity in all our children, and give them the confidence and space to pursue their passions.

Attention is now focused on a more diverse education landscape and providing greater flexibility and choice for students. The Integrated Programmes, for example, allowed some students to skip the O-Level examinations, so that time and space could be made available for more enriching educational activities. Lines between different secondary school courses were blurred, allowing students in the Normal (Academic) or N(A) course to offer up to two O-Level subjects and those in the Normal (T) course to take up to two N(A) subjects. More options were injected into the examination system by encouraging some schools to propose new O-Level subjects such as Drama, whilst others partner the polytechnics to offer Applied Subjects. These options

[1] Speech by Mr Tharman Shanmugaratnam, Acting Minister for Education, at the appointment ceremony for principals, 30 December 2003.

enriched the examination system further by expanding the choice of subjects. The revised A-Level curriculum represented yet another significant change, with subjects pitched at three levels — H1, H2 and H3. Various modes of H3 subjects were also introduced, with some offered by local universities. Changes in the A-Level curriculum and examination were intended to provide students with a broad-based curriculum that emphasised the inter-connections between disciplines. The revised curriculum was also aimed at nurturing their thinking and communication skills.

Undoubtedly, the changing needs and demands of Singapore have transformed the educational landscape from a collection of disparate systems to a cohesive and well-regarded education system. Underlying these structural changes, however, are strands of continuity that laid a strong foundation, upon which the changes in education and examinations are continuously made.

CONTINUITY

Examinations remain a key element of Singapore's changing education landscape. This is because examinations serve several key functions — from certifying the achievement of students to providing critical information on how well the education system is functioning. Institutions of higher learning use examination results to select students while employers depend on them in recruiting staff. For the government, information on the level of student participation in examinations and their level of achievement indicate the state of health of the education system. Public confidence in examinations is therefore critical and this depends on three key aspects of examinations — validity, reliability and fairness.

While the form of examinations may have changed over time, the need to ensure these three key aspects of examinations is paramount if examination results are to be relied on for various purposes. Achieving validity, reliability and fairness hinge on several factors, ranging from the design of examination questions to the administration of examinations. In this regard, it is heartening to note that even for the Sime Road School Certificate examination, proper procedures were followed to ensure validity, reliability and fairness. Questions were set by internees who served in the Malayan Education Service prior to the war. Examination papers were typed in secrecy and sealed in envelopes to preserve confidentiality.

The handling of the 1961 examination boycott exemplified the importance attached to validity, reliability and fairness of examinations. The Ministry of Education (MOE) introduced several measures to ensure this — from the setting up of emergency examination centres for candidates who could not take the examination in their own school due to picket lines to the provision of supplementary examinations for those who missed the examination. In the marking of scripts, the Ministry took into account the unfavourable conditions under which candidates took the examination.

Throughout the period of change in education, examinations continued to play its role in certifying the achievement of students. For this to be possible, there is a need to maintain the credibility of examinations, so that users of examination results and certificates have confidence in them. Regardless of the form of examination, whether it was the Cambridge School Certificate, or the Government Secondary IV School Certificate (Chinese), there were established procedures to mark scripts and set appropriate standards.

The high level of public confidence in Singapore's national examination is a tribute to generations of examination personnel, working tirelessly behind the scenes to ensure that examinations are valid, reliable and fair. Examination personnel go to great lengths to ensure that all candidates have a fair shot at examinations, including the provision of Braille and enlarged print for the visually impaired to the conduct of examinations in hospitals for candidates who were unwell but otherwise fit to sit for examinations. Even the outbreak of the Severe Acute Respiratory Syndrome (SARS) in 2003 did not stop examinations. Instead, special arrangements were made to ensure that examinations continue, including temperature screening and the provision of special rooms for candidates with minor ailments.

While each change in education and examination necessitates corresponding changes in examinations, the key principles underlying a good examination have stood the test of time.

CONCLUSION

The history of examinations has attested to the contributions of both change and continuity — concomitantly, both would leave legacies for the generations of Singaporeans to come.

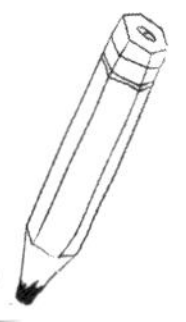